The Best of Apfelbaum's Corner

Earl P. L. Apfelbaum

The Best of Apfelbaum's Corner

A Collection of
Articles
by
Earl P. L. Apfelbaum

Copyright © 1983 by Earl P. L. Apfelbaum, Inc.
All Rights Reserved
Library of Congress Catalog Card No. 83-91066
Printed in the United States of America
by
Dorrance & Company, Inc.
Bryn Mawr, Pennsylvania 19010

PREFACE

Stamp collecting began within a few months of the first use of postage stamps to prepay the carrying of mail. That event was in the year of 1840 in Great Britain. A general reformation of postal service was long overdue and the invention of stamps was the catalyst that brought it about. In the intervening 140 years stamps have spread to all nations and every corner of the earth. They have served well in the spread of education, the expansion of business and the increase of social contacts. They are truly one of the great inventions of all times.

From the time of my childhood I have collected stamps. Their fascination for me led to a desire to devote my life to philately, the word coined from Greek to be applied to the general subject of studying and gathering things that pertain to or are part of mail service. Therefore, when in 1930 economic conditions forced me together with my father, Maurice J. Apfelbaum, to find a new occupation, I turned to a philatelic career with joy. While the path to the present has had its rough times and periods of struggle I have never regretted the decision.

Now about these short articles that constitute this book. They started in 1963 as a result of observing how similar writings used by a Philadelphia automobile dealer had had positive public relations effect. After talking the matter over with our advertising agency we decided to insert an essay in Linn's Weekly Stamp News and Stamp Collector each week. The essays were to be eighty percent or more pointed to the popularization of philately. They received the column heading "Apfelbaum's Corner."

The fear at first was that I would run out of ideas after a few months but so wide is the scope of the stamp collecting hobby that I am still going strong after twenty years. Any idea that causes collectors to think about their avocation is good because even if they have reached a lukewarm stage in their interest it brings to their mind some related part of the hobby that they have enjoyed. The thousands of letters I have received from readers repeat over and over how much their stamp collecting has been similar to the kinds I comment on.

Books of this type are the kind a reader nibbles on—a bit here and a bit there. You can open it to the middle before reading the first page. They are a source of pleasure at all parts.

I wish to acknowledge the fine assistance my grandson, John Apfelbaum, has given me in selecting and editing these articles.

Earl P.L. Apfelbaum
Philadelphia 1983

INTRODUCTION

Every business day I write from twenty to fifty letters almost all dealing with particular matters between my firm and the addressee. This leaves little or no time to carry on personal correspondence. The estimated fifty to one hundred thousand stamp collectors I have met and invariably liked well enough to desire continual contact must be almost completely left out of the wonderful personal touch that letters permit. There just isn't time.

This column is the nearest thing to letters that I have been able to devise. Through it I reach thousands whom I know, and additional thousands whom I would like to know. Each week as thoughts strike me, I can express them briefly in letter form and broadcast them over America hoping they will be widely read. That they are is evident from the hundreds of communications I receive from readers.

My personal contact with collectors has been over an area equal to half our globe. It is my extreme pleasure to continue talking to them all weekly via *Apfelbaum's Corner*.

* * *

Labor Day of 1930 marked the dividing point of public opinion as to whether "Hoover's Depression" was to be a big bump or a careening cataclysm rapidly getting out of control. On this eventful day my father, Maurice, and I embarked on an enterprise intended to provide the proverbial roof over our heads and destined to become life work for both of us: a stamp business.

We opened our first stamp shop in a small, third-floor walk-up office in a building at the southeast corner of 10th and Chestnut Streets in Philadelphia. Dad's and my personal collections, plus $500.00 borrowed from insurance companies financed the purchase of fixtures, signs, advertising—and paid the rent for awhile too.

Business was hardly what you could call good. Even so, the market for stamps was much better than those for diamonds, first editions, autographs and other collectable valuables. Stamp collectors retained their interest in the hobby and continued to purchase needed materials though, of course, in much smaller amounts than in the years prior to 1929.

One big help to us then, as now, was the fact that we dealt in and stocked stamps of all countries and times. We weren't as subject to the fluctuations caused by the rise and fall of specialties as were many dealers at that time and even today. And we were lucky too. At low points in our venture, something always turned up—a "good buy" or a commission to handle the liquidation of a valuable property.

In 1933 we were able to move to a slightly larger, street level store at 52 North 11th Street. We stayed at this location for eleven years, catering to a local trade on the limited scale of such stores.

Our first few years in the stamp business weren't as bad as the several that followed. In 1934 we started our public auctions and seemed to be gaining some slight momentum. Then my father died. It was probably the greatest personal tragedy I have ever suffered. His loss affected me for some time, and with general business conditions growing worse by the day, it seemed for awhile that our little stamp shop wasn't going to make it.

With a lot of help from friends and family, we managed to pull through. Soon we began to get a little bigger. We grew slowly at first. Then a little faster. Today we are growing so rapidly that it is almost impossible to believe such progress possible.

I often think back to those early "depression" years. They were hardly the fondest I have spent, but they did teach me a great lesson that, I think, has helped me to keep my feet on the ground during the wonderful years we are now experiencing.

It may seem strange to you, but I still get a pins-and-needles tingle every time I compare that first 225 square-foot store to what I have now. It's a good feeling.

* * *

We have been asked, "Why do you care what kind of stamp shops there are available to collectors other than your own?"

We care because the only way we can keep our hobby growing is by making comfortable, well stocked and pleasantly conducted stamp stores available to collectors. There are many people who do not wish to do business by mail. These are people who, for various reasons, prefer to do business in person, or face-to-face. We care about the facilities of other stamp shops because they reflect a marked image on stamp collecting in general.

We want people to be collectors, and if it requires that good competitive stores be established in Paducah, Columbia and Boise, then that's fine with us.

We, as all dealers with modern and efficient facilities, profit from the collective health of philately. We endorse any and all efforts others make to improving the facilities for stamp buying and selling.

* * *

With the coming of Spring, we resume our "road work". No, this isn't an athletic endeavor. This is travel to view collections that are for sale. Within the next six months we expect to cover 30,000 miles of North American highways, calling on philatelists in their homes or offices to either purchase or arrange for the sale of their collections. In this, we have what is probably the world's most pleasant occupation.

During the years since 1930, when we first started taking to the highways and byways, we have met and done business with thousands of collectors. With but a few exceptions, our services have pleased them. After all, no one can please the fellow who buys second class stamps with the idea that some fool dealer will later on take them off his hands as superb copies.

By far the majority of those selling understand the basic economic fact that they will only receive the wholesale value of their material because the purchasing dealer has expenses and a profit to make. They know that some stamps are more popular than others and have a better market value. They realize that five and ten cent items are available in the trade at per hundred and per thousand prices and so will hardly be figured when the overall estimate of a collection is made. They also appreciate that the care they lavished on their collection adds to its value when selling. Dealers are only able to complete transactions with sellers who understand these economic imperatives.

* * *

"Mr. X" is collecting Missouri postal history. "Mr. Y" is as keen for Montana. Then there is a long line of people after everything from Hong Kong to Tenerife. Our hope is to always have as much available in each of these lines as our friends have money to spend for their specialty. Alas, in philately it cannot be.

There is no philatelic field other than the new issue business (and even that has exceptions) where the supply of merchandise is unlimited. Some subjects are so limited as to have practically no commercial supply except when a former collector places his material on the market. Needless to say, this is gobbled up in a short time and once again the market is dry.

There is a group of specialities that have a more generous floating inventory in dealer's hands. Generally they are from countries or areas that had high economic and cultural development during the time of the specialty. England and France during the Nineteenth century, and parts of Italy during the Eighteenth century are examples. While there are many scarce items from each of these countries, so much was created that a huge reservoir of material currently exists.

Collectors who seek specialties should give long consideration to their choice of subjects. Most important should be whether they want to fish in a well-stocked lake or cast their line in a stream that only occasionally has a fish.

* * *

I recently flew from Chicago to Philadelphia in one hour and twenty minutes. Only a few years ago it took a sixteen hour train ride to cover the same distance. Of course, the plane is by comparison a modern miracle. But what has been accomplished by me with the more than half a day saved? Am I putting my newly added time to good purpose? I confess I am in doubt.

On the train I had leisure to think. Because I had to ride for an extended period of time I could undertake reading a long book or writing a short story which I had carried in my mind for some time. Occasionally along the way I met interesting fellow travelers, and was with them long enough to benefit from their conversation and knowledge. In good weather, the passing landscape was of interest and sometimes it even inspired a lyric in my thoughts.

Now one scarcely unfastens the seat belt when the light flashes, "fasten seat belts," for landing. Then begins the rush to home or office, the resumption of our briefly interrupted routine. There is no thought of abstract things, no reserve of composure accumulated for tomorrow.

Is it any wonder that every day more and more people are turning to stamp collecting as one of the few remaining calming influences in life? Philately is both tonic and restorant for the jaded and tired mind. It is a place in life to day-dream. It is for many, all that remains which they themselves truly control.

* * *

Mortality in the stamp business is said to be higher than in other lines of business. A check of the advertisers in this paper compared with those of five years ago will well prove the point. If one goes back ten, twenty or thirty years, it will be difficult to find many firms that have survived the years with an unbroken business record.

One reason for the high death rate is that few stamp dealers build an organization that will continue on after them. For the most part they conduct a solitary or a mom-and-pop type business. This accounts for the ending of many illustrious professional philatelic names.

We believe that a good business reputation and useful service should be continued through the years under management that has grown up with the business, and takes over as the older executives retire or pass on.

* * *

Recently, I heard a man who claimed over forty years of collecting, tell members of a club that they should never spend a cent for anything but United States stamps, and they should always be sure that the postal clerk gives them a plate number with each purchase.

There are similarly misguided exponents of First Day Covers, British colonies, Latin America and all other collecting fields. There are those who expound loud and long on the merits of no hinges, sheet collecting, used only, unused only, printed albums, blank albums, rarities, cheap stamps, etc.—in fact, almost anything one can think of in connection with stamp collecting.

Advice that tends to take away from anyone the possibility of the fullest enjoyment of our hobby is narrow thinking. Collectors should be free to save what they like to save, not what some self-designated expert advises. If Afghanistan is interesting and one wants stamps from there, it doesn't matter a bit if no one else locally is interested. In fact, stamp collecting will profit in any community from a diversity of collecting interest of local collectors.

Broad studies by economists have proven that increase in worth or scarcity of stamps is not limited to any type, country, or group of issues. Prizes in shows are as often given for so called unpopular as popular subjects.

Philately is big. Its followers, on the whole, are big people who want to know and thrill to more than a small segment of its scope. We cater to all stamp collecting interests and encourage ventures into any phase of this great hobby.

* * *

There aren't many collectors today who would remember my father. This is their loss, because in today's hectic world it is a novelty to find a person like him.

Spending an hour with a new collector, man or boy, instructing in the "house" of philately, was far more important to my father than selling a hundred valuable stamps. By telling one of his endless, inimitable anecdotes, he could kindle the flame in any novice collector. His philosophy, that life was more than seeking an ever bigger business and increasing wealth, could well be reconsidered today.

Nevertheless, just as my father was patient and understanding with new and appreciative philatelists, he was perturbed and annoyed by the silliness and nonsense that has always attached itself to the hem of philately.

My father was for stamp collecting, for fun and for learning. He could never understand why anyone would want to introduce the worries of speculation, the responsibilities of influencing our Post Office Department, and the undue concern over pristine gum into our otherwise unblemished hobby. He would be aghast at some of today's schemes to promote even more needless issues.

We are proud that in our formative years, we had such a head of our business.

* * *

One of the loneliest times in life is the period just after a loved husband or wife has passed away. It then seems that nothing is worth doing. Days become full of emptiness. Remorse and self-pity frequently get the upperhand.

All too often, the greatest therapy in this trying situation is overlooked. If the deceased mate pursued a hobby, then this is the time for the remaining spouse to actively continue that hobby. The intense absorption that was there for one can usually be found by the other.

If the hobby was stamp-collecting, there is always some phase of the collection in which the survivor can discover interest, and in addition to the pleasure of associating with objects that meant so much to the deceased spouse, there is the gratifying feeling of continuing, and perhaps successfully finishing the project.

This leads me to the point of this article. Widows and widowers shouldn't rush to dispose of a stamp collection immediately upon the death of their spouse.

Retain it for a while...at least until it is definitely known that it will not be a desired and useful treasure worth far more, as a pleasurable time consumer and companion, than the monetary return that it may bring.

* * *

Stamp exhibitions need an addition to their classifications, because at present they ignore the largest body of collectors: those with general collections mounted in printed albums.

Let's face facts. More people collect in printed than blank albums, and are general or one-of-a-kind collectors, rather than specialists. More people understand this form of collecting better than any other. Yet when clubs or societies stage stamp exhibitions, all but the specialists are frozen out in the classification of entries and the awards made by juries.

Is it any wonder then that the millions of "outside" collectors don't attend stamp shows or take an interest in clubs. We make them feel like "step-children".

We need a place in every show where these printed albums with their general assemblages of stamps can be entered. We need awards for worthy efforts in this category. We also need judges with an appreciation for the more generalized stamp collecting interests of these millions of people.

The fact that these millions don't find twenty varieties where Scott only finds one shouldn't freeze them out of the shows.

* * *

Rarely will you find perfection in the work of man. All things we make or do have their faults. Certainly stamps, stamp collecting and stamp dealing are no exceptions.

The tolerance that others expect for their less-than-perfect work is sought just as much by stamp dealers. They can only sell the stamps that a country has produced. If a country printed an issue on poor quality paper with fugitive ink and poorly perforated, that's the way it is.

The occasional stamp collector who insists on perfection rarely has a collection that would fill a shoe box. Most certainly he can't have a collection that is a true reflection of stamps as they are produced.

We believe in nice quality in stamps. Dirty, torn, frousy and tired copies don't appeal to us, and we don't care to sell them.

We do sell sound stamps that are attractive, desirable and collectable. And best of all, they are representative of what the country has issued as postage for the delivery of mail.

* * *

The McGraw-Hill Publishing Company, one of the world's leading publishers of business magazines, recently conducted a survey of philately in the United States. The survey doesn't present any startling or hitherto unknown information about our hobby, but actually confirms the "off-the-cuff" deductions that many dealers and professionals have been making through the years.

However, of far more importance than the data the report presents, is the fact that a "giant" of the publishing industry should recognize the popularity of philately—and spend the time and money for further investigation.

Through the years we have watched philately grow and prosper in an almost unpredictable fashion. And we are still excited when someone outside our philatelic world peeks in at us to take a look.

For instance, a short time ago, we announced the purchase of a rather valuable and important collection. When this information reached local newspapers and radio stations, reporters kept us busy for hours answering many questions about the purchase and about philately. One local TV station even filmed the collection on its arrival at our offices, and later showed the film on their evening news program because they estimated that their audience contained over 250,000 stamp enthusiasts.

Admittedly, we were somewhat flustered by this rash of interest. It kept our staff humming for days. But we welcomed the chance to display philately and ourselves to those who might be interested. This is the only way that philately will continue to grow and prosper, and this is important to every collector and dealer.

* * *

Stamp auctions have been developing as a form of stamp merchandising for close to a century.

The catalogs of the first auctions were no more than listings of the stamps to be sold. Condition wasn't mentioned because it wasn't of importance. All that the buyer expected was a stamp. Its qualities didn't count.

Today, of course, it's quite different. The best copies bring the highest prices, and sometimes a phenomenal example of a stamp sells for a truly amazing price. This is as it should be.

The honest auction describer should, in a detached way, gauge the quality of what he sells, and without undue flourish (unless truly deserved) write his description. To do this requires experience and philatelic ability. The indiscriminate use of terms such as "superb," "unique," "only as one other known," or other epithets cheapens such terms unless they may be justly applied to worthy material.

Of course it isn't long before buyers become acutely aware of those who overdescribe. In the meantime, however, damage is done to buyers who accept the seller's grading without question.

* * *

It has always been our opinion that stamp collectors get the most fun out of arranging their own collections. However, some years ago we had a client with a different opinion. He brought his albums into our office one day and said that he had fifty dollars a month to spend on them. Would we take care of it for him? Of course we would. But when he started to leave without the albums, the true meaning of his request became clear. He intended that we place his collection in our safes and once each month we were to add fifty dollars worth of stamps of our own choosing to them. He in turn would send us payment on the first of each month. This arrangement went on for several years until the gentleman retired from business. What fun he got from his collection we never learned.

* * *

For the sake of future generations of collectors, let's take better care of the stamps we have. Let's avoid those practices which might further diminish our already vanishing supplies of desirable stamps.

Let's think twice before buying cheap album paper that contains strong chemicals. Let's be more cautious in the use of tight, damaging mounts. Let's ensure that our stamps will not suffer from dirty fingers and rough handling. In areas of excessive heat and humidity, like Florida and the Gulf Coast States, let's provide properly air-conditioned rooms for preserving unused stamps with gum.

We cannot be overly cautious in our care of stamps, if we hope to preserve for the future the tie with history that our philatelic possessions constitute.

Perhaps the time will come when in order to have any examples at all of certain perishable stamps we will have to set up a standard of values based on the extent of repair they possess. It should be possible with care to defer this time.

Let's all exercise the needed care.

* * *

When I asked a fine elderly gentleman in Wisconsin the price he expected for his collection he said $7861.42. Somewhat surprised at such exact figures, I inquired how he had decided on it. His answer was, "I kept an accurate account of what I spent for them and this is exactly what I want back."

I have no fault to find with a person trying to sell at whatever price he decides on. However, I would like to mention a few factors that should be considered in arriving at a price.

First in importance is the matter of the market at the time of selling. It may be higher or lower than when the material was purchased.

Second is the question of the popularity of the material involved. Plate number blocks or red cancellations may have been the rage when the collection was being formed but, as in all things, styles change in philately, too.

Third, the right dealer must be approached. Some dealers are too highly specialized, others too small, etc. to handle every philatelic property offered.

Fourth, consideration must be made for the long, pleasant, educational and therapeutic benefits that have been received from forming the collection. These are usually a bargain if figured at as much as fifty percent of what the stamps cost you.

* * *

Do you have trouble getting the stamps you want? I think it's good if you do. When stamp collecting becomes too easy it loses its hold on its followers. That is why those who buy only new issues drop by the wayside in such large numbers. There must be some difficulty, and a little delay between the wanting and getting of a stamp to key up the excitement of its being acquired.

Going to the post office for the latest issue doesn't give much of this pleasure. On the other hand, bidding in auctions before winning a wanted item is sure to keep any collector anxious and give him a thrill when the desired piece is finally won.

Try to get this kind of thrill in your collecting efforts. Someday, you may recall it as your greatest return from philately.

* * *

Almost every hobby depends for its major support on the middle-income class. Even in the United States, the upper-income level is too small numerically to provide an active market for such lively pursuits as philately, numismatics and other popular avocations.

For example, Mexico is a country with a relatively small middle-income group, and the collecting of stamps "south of the border" is generally restricted to a handful of the wealthier populace and the rich "foreign colony."

Consequently, successful stamp dealing in Mexico is on a very small scale. Good stocks are almost nonexistent and the only encouragement the hobby gets is through a few packet displays in Mexico City.

Large stamp firms make many sales of $1000 and more. They need big sales to help support their wide-spread business. They like well-to-do customers. Nevertheless, without the thousands of middle-income, smaller buyers they and the rest of philately would soon be below the horizon of recognition as the world's greatest hobby.

* * *

How far is it from an initial collecting effort to a full experience of the pleasures of stamp collecting? No distance at all. Unlike most other hobbies, a stamp collector experiences all the thrills and pleasures right from the beginning.

True, the enjoyment continues for as long as he collects, but for him there was no waiting. Each new acquisition, every examination of a stamp, and all the minutes spent with them have "paid off," in relaxed and painless learning.

The collection itself may have great or little philatelic value. The builder may even be uninformed about the regular methods of collecting. Still he enjoys it.

The mystical factors that make up our fascinating pursuit are difficult to pin down. Let it be sufficient that they are there and that we all gain from them in the way most suited to our individual temperaments. So long as this is so, the future of stamp collecting is assured.

* * *

In reviewing and examining the many hundreds of stamp collections throughout a year, we are often struck with the high frequency of "sameness" of collections. This is not to find fault with those who like to patronize the post office, be it Uncle Sam's or those of other nations. It just seems to me that this method of collecting is much too easy, and for that reason one can lose interest too soon. For a hobby to be interesting and absorbing, it should present a challenge in order to hold the adult mind.

Delving into stamps of the past is usually no more expensive than buying those of the present. But it is much more exciting, educational, and presents greater opportunity for recovery if ever the collection is sold.

The Eighteen-hundreds and early Nineteen-hundreds had all the problems of postal service we have now, and some that we no longer have. The post offices existent in 1903 are likely to be more alluring than those of today. Finding covers with cancels from that or any other earlier period can be loads of fun and certainly can be written up in an album with more individualism than can a collection of today's made to order covers.

The same goes for stamps, cancellation collections and even the fascinating sidelines of revenues, postal stationery, etc.

It isn't necessary to be rich, artistic or learned to enjoy older issues. All that is required is a desire to get the most fun for your money.

* * *

Copying Bill Veeck's theory that baseball is for the "Little guy," I think that stamp collecting is millions of little guys having fun, getting thrills and hoping for the extra enjoyment in life that we all seek.

By little guys I don't mean men of small stature, kids, or people with tiny brains. I mean the average fellow who works hard, has to budget closely, and dreams of things he would have if the boss suddenly became more liberal. The wife and kids have a first lien on everything he makes and whenever a wedge is cut out of the bank account for stamps, he stands naked before the judgement of his conscience.

To this "little guy" stamp collecting owes its biggest debt. He supports its clubs, its national societies, and its dealers. He is the one who makes it a multi-million dollar business. He is the one who recruits its new followers and acts as its public relations agent. To him we owe much.

Let's start repaying the "little guy." The way to do this is to make it more fun for him to acquire stamps, to give him greater pleasure to own them, and less pain to part with them when the time comes.

Let's spruce up stamp dealing, particularly in its selling, with attractive merchandising quarters and ample stocks to select from. Let's put new gimmicks into stamp shows to make them as exciting as a circus. Finally, let's cut out the bunk and hokum about disposing of your collection for a huge profit when we know that many collectors pay for their pleasure by selling for less than it cost them. The truth always is best. A change in "wanted to buy" advertising is called for so that our "little guy" will realistically buy, enjoy, and sell with the advance knowledge that every stamp or cover isn't an Eldorado.

* * *

Nicaragua, Bolivia and Paraguay are not the most popular countries, philatelically. They take a place far to the rear of France, Germany, and Great Britain. This comes about naturally because few collectors have either ancestral ties to these lands, or are concerned with, or have an economic interest in these countries.

However, when it comes to getting fun from collecting, the Nicaragua, Bolivia and Paraguay boys have it all over the followers of the popular cults. They collect in a realm where varieties, both listed and unlisted, abound; where for a few dollars one can get really rare stamps, and where the catalog can be thrown out of the window to let personal fancy determine degree, direction and diversity of philatelic accomplishment. It is practically impossible for a collector to be original or to make a find in one of the popular countries. It is equally difficult for a collector to miss these thrill givers when assembling a Nicaragua collection, or, to a lesser degree, miss turning up interesting items in an assemblage of Paraguay or Bolivia.

Many minor varieties of these countries came about for the simple reason that the printers couldn't read or couldn't find sufficient type of the same font to arrange a complete setting. These are good practical reasons for errors and varieties.

* * *

A comic once said, "People have more fun than anybody!" We think stamp dealers have more fun than anybody. The dealer not only has unlimited hours for his hobby, he also has the opportunity to meet and make friends with many collectors. He sees their collections under conditions that are more relaxed and conducive to enjoyment than are afforded by the best exhibitions. Further, the dealer is granted that greatest of all bequests, the privilege of proselytizing for a cause that he believes in.

Stamps dealers receive a special joy from new collectors. Every time a convert is added to the fold, the responsible dealer feels pride in his accomplishment. Stamp dealers can choose to merchandise the stamps they like best, and thus enjoy to the fullest the arranging, study, and handling of their pets. They can, and most often do, get to know their clients both commercially and socially. The fraternizing of philatelists is usually on a high level and not marred by prejudices of race, religion, or economic status.

With all of these advantages, I believe the stamp dealer "has more fun than anybody." But there is plenty of fun left for the collector. Any professional dealer will be delighted to show you how to get more fun out of life.

* * *

In news reports of auction prices realized, we rarely learn what percentage of overall catalog value a collection has brought. Certain prime pieces are selected for reporting. But what is really important to the owner, "how much it all came to," is ignored.

Any good stamp auction house can get high prices for selected rarities of exceptional quality. This is of little consequence to most collectors because such items constitute a small proportion of the total catalog value of their collections. The real point to concentrate on is, *what the auction house can get for more ordinary stamps and covers.*

For years the best auctioneers have realized that the seller is best pleased by realizing for him a higher amount for all of his consignment than he expected. Of course he wants his pet pieces to sell well, but money in the bank is measured by the height of the balance, not little parts of what is there.

* * *

It is now close to twenty years since any United States stamp issue of this century became even semi-scarce. In most cases the stamps of this time period are available from dealers for little more than face value. Dealers have the continual problem of liquidating huge amounts of the material to business houses for use as postage. Of course, this must be done at a discount from face value which can range as high as twenty percent off for some items.

Despite these facts, there are still many people laying away sheets of current issues hopeful that in the future they will return a profit. Such a profit is extremely unlikely in our lifetime. How much better off these people would be if they only purchased the single, block or plate block their collection requires and then spent the difference for a variety of stamps from bygone years that have already achieved a premium value.

They then would be buying real philatelic worth that would not be likely to decrease because such stamps are in ever diminishing supply for an ever expanding market. Instead of money tied up in duplication they would have a collection of broader scope and certainly of more interest to any prospective buyer at some future date.

* * *

Has your exhibition committee applied for the "Maurice Apfelbaum Award For Excellence in Stamp Collecting?" The award, an attractive 2-1/2 inch gold medallion, is made available without charge to any stamp show that includes a special category for collections displayed on regular printed album pages in its prospectus.

Our purpose in offering the award is to make stamp exhibitions more interesting for the millions of collectors who use Scott, Minkus, White Ace and other printed albums. At present these collectors are practically disregarded by show committees and judges.

It is not our intention to depreciate the value of specialization, individual write-up and unusual presentations. We think these activities are excellent and encourage them. However, we also want to encourage the vast number of collectors who do not, and perhaps never will, collect that way. The "printed album collectors" are important to philately, and this is our way of welcoming them into philatelic circles and providing a place for them in our stamp shows.

* * *

Very little has been written on the subject of "The Law and Philately." One legal guide to buying and selling stamps, however, is well established by court decisions. The courts have ruled that stamp dealers are responsible for what they sell.

In other words, stamps must be, in regard to authenticity, quality and identification, exactly what the dealer has described them to be. This means that responsibility rests on every stamp merchant, whether large or small, expert or novice, to be familiar with everything he buys or sells.

Consider this well. Is this the reason why so many of the newer dealers only advertise recent issues which usually do not require much study and research?

* * *

By now it should be evident that there will never be an end to the special events that cause the issuance of stamps. The New York World's Fair is the latest of these motivations for special issues, and for the information by many collectors of so-called "limited" Topical Collections.

To many people, history is only enjoyed as it unfolds in their daily newspapers. Thus, the formation of current history collections that have to do with the Geophysical Year, the Marian Year, the Brussels Fair and a host of other recent historical topics is widespread.

We wish these collectors well, and certainly won't suggest that they change their stamp collecting habits. However, there are pitfalls that I feel obliged to call to their attention.

First, and most important, beware of stamps that are issued in a controlled fashion that makes it impossible to determine their actual value.

Second, understand that the important minor variety of today will be almost completely neglected by the time the next topic comes along.

Third, realize that the stamps you are buying for your current topic are also being bought in huge quantities by many other collectors. The passage of time and the popularity of the next current topic will inevitably make these stamps surplus in a depressed market.

There are exceptions to these rules, of course, but not in sufficient number to prompt any thinking person to collect these current topical issues for gains other than pleasure and education.

* * *

There are mathematical systems for determining what stamps will become rare or advance in price each year. There are theories covering the value of all stamps at any future period, and there are promoters selling stamps solely on the basis that they are clever enough to pick the good ones for clients who are certain to reap a financial windfall if they follow this advice.

I say "bosh" to all these. I have been in the stamp business for fifty years and have seen soothsayers, sophists and shrewdies come and go — but never last. They can't last because it takes only a few years to show the best of them up.

The imponderables in philately such as styles of collecting, popularity of issues and countries at various times, economic factors, cupidity of individual promoters — these and many more cannot be incorporated into sound theories or mathematical formulas.

The only sure way to gain a profit from stamp collecting is to enjoy the hobby as you go along. Then, regardless of what the future brings, you must come out ahead.

* * *

Many people look forward to retirement as a time when they will be able to collect or deal in stamps. From experience, I must report that the great majority of those who postpone philatelic activity until the sunset of life never get to it. The stamp collecting habit should be enjoyed now, if it appeals to you.

Perhaps, because of the pressure of business or child rearing, the time available now is limited. But by all means, if you like philately, squeeze out a little time for it daily. Then, when retirement comes, the stamp collecting habit will be well established as a continuing pleasure in life.

For those who are burdened with extra expenses while sending John and Maria through college, there are hundreds of by ways of stamp collecting that cost very little. For those who moonlight with an extra job, what's better than an inside coat pocket collection that can be enjoyed at opportune moments.

You are living now, and at best the future is uncertain, so if you hope to be a stamp collector, get at it today. The benefits it offers may not be postponed without the chance of missing them altogether.

* * *

I recently visited Arizona, and found that the people there are most concerned about their lack of abundant water. Their state is growing fast, but unless their water supply problem is soon solved, it will limit their potential population.

What has this to do with philately? Nothing, except that stamps can be used to inform people of the possible solution to this problem. Postage stamps are a fine medium of education and publicity.

Instead of the endless stream of memorial and commemorative stamps that we issue, there could be a series devoted to the engineering that will someday bring more water to our west.

Sooner or later, we will have to tap the great river and lake systems of Northern Canada and Alaska to bring bloom to our parched areas. Now is the time to tell our people how it will be done and what it will cost.

There is no better medium than postage stamps to put over that proposal.

* * *

During the period from 1890-1900, the stamp catalogs of the world dropped the listing of postal stationery. This was not because collectors of the day had lost interest in that segment of the hobby. It was because dealers and cataloguers believed that the requisite number of philatelic varieties required to maintain a good volume of business had been reached. And they believed that the space devoted to postal stationery listings could be saved without hurting philately.

Over the intervening years, several new crops of collectors have been on the scene, and philately has changed from a game of seeing who can get the most stamps, to one of using stamps for research into all phases of life.

Postal stationery is frequently artistic and always as historically significant as the stamps of a country. It is a branch of philately worthy of your interest.

New catalogs which cover the subject of postal stationery are now appearing. Rarities can still be purchased as sleepers.

* * *

Common sense is all that is required to quash some of the sillyisms of stamp collecting. A case in point is embraced in the collection of the United States Columbian issue of 1893. Of the dollar values, the $1 was issued in the largest quantity (55,050); the $4 in the smallest (26,350).

Many of these stamps were used for postage and were thus lost to collectors by destruction. Of the used examples that were saved, many were heavily cancelled or damaged in the mails.

The unused specimens that collectors of that day saved were placed in their collections with hinges, as was the custom then and is still today among many philatelists. The only dollar Columbians that were not so treated were the small number that were duplicates of the day and were purchased with the idea of being useful for future trading. During the more than 20 year period when the stamps sold below face value, much of the duplicate stock was sold to business houses and was used on registered mail and parcels.

Now, some ninety years later, it is rare indeed to find any completely sound Columbians in an unused condition. In all that expanse of time it is estimated that stamps of this issue would have been in at least 16 different collections! To expect to find any of these stamps with full original gum and never having been hinged, is to expect a miracle. If, in all the world there are 500 such stamps, it would be amazing. Certainly many exist with the old gum washed off and new glue applied. We are not, however referring to such stamps.

Despite the history of this issue, within a recent week, eight different collectors turned down dollar Columbians in our retail department because they had been hinged!

Of course, the price that never-hinged, full original gum Columbians should carry would have surprised these shoppers. If you consider the history of the Columbians and the mathematical probabilities for obtaining perfect unused specimens you can probably estimate their value. To have such perfect stamps readily available at popular prices would mean developing a stamp fixing process to make possible what cannot exist without tampering.

* * *

A stamp dealer that I know gave up smoking last year. The reason for giving up the habit was due to a costly accident. He had just sold a valuable air mail stamp to a client, and as he was holding it in his tweezers preparing to put it into a plastic mount, sparks from his cigarette fell on the stamp. One spark burned a tiny hole in it. And the stamp's value was instantly reduced by more than a thousand dollars!

I never cease to be amazed at people who handle their stamp collections while smoking. We find repeated evidence of fine stamps that are either soiled by tobacco ashes or are made almost valueless because of ash burns from cigarettes, cigars or pipes.

This is not a plea to stop smoking. Smoke, if you like, but please guard your stamps from dangerous, destructive ashes, both hot and cold.

* * *

We have all met fanatics: people who only think and talk about one subject. It might be baseball, religion, politics, their ailments or stamp collecting. Sometimes on the first meeting they are interesting. But after a while we invariably try to avoid them because we know they will be boring.

In a stamp club, the fellow who will only discuss his specialty is soon the one we don't want to sit next to. It is good to know one subject well, but most of us have more general interests. It is fortunate that only a few of us blind ourselves to the fascination of everything else in life.

All philately is interesting, be it the seeking of plate flaws on a stamp issued in 1850, or the use of an encyclopedia to better understand the subject on the newest issue of Tunisia.

None of us has the time to do all things. But, when we can see or hear about subjects beyond our own fields of activity, it is good for us to do so. The culture of our times calls for the intellectual man to both specialize and generalize. His specialty is for the advancement of particular learning. His generalizing is to more fully understand and appreciate life.

* * *

When a stamps collector dies, his collection dies, his collection must be appraised in order to set its value for estate and inheritance tax purposes. This is a task that should only be entrusted to professional philatelists who are familiar with the type of collection involved and its market value.

On hundreds of occasions we have seen long typewritten lists of the contents of a collection that listed every last two-cent item in the collection. The preparation of these lists are not only real labor, but the fruits of the labor are absolutely meaningless.

What is needed is a professional evaluation of what a collection can be sold for. This is rarely catalog value. Professional appraisers will value the collection by the worth of the material of value that is included in the property.

Knowledgeable buyers will never pay more than so-much-per-hundred or so-much-per-thousand for very low valued or common material. They do pay good prices for scarce items and material in demand.

The important point is, when the dealer prepares his estimate of value for lawyers, executors, trust officers or other interested persons, his appraisal should be almost on the "nose" as to what can be realized through a sale.

* * *

A nickle trolley ride would have gotten you to the old Philadelphia Stamp Club back in 1920. The Club—as everyone called it—met every Tuesday and Friday evening and Saturday afternoon. Its meeting room had several long tables, about fifty chairs, the omnipresent cuspidors, and an inordinately thick layer of cigar smoke when the crowd gathered.

The Club was centrally located and, since suburban living hadn't as yet robbed the city of many of its upper classes, its membership included a goodly number of the society and millionaire strata. There were easily a dozen successful stamp shops in Philadelphia at that time and each of these merchants felt it his responsibility to belong to and sustain the Club. The Club had no competition because there was no need for it.

Meetings of the old Philadelphia Stamp Club usually attracted from fifty to one hundred people. They assembled to talk, trade and trump one another's stories of finds. Almost everyone collected the world, and needed stamps from every country. Almost everyone would swap Zanzibar for Canada as readily as they would cut a pair of imperforates to make the single they needed in their albums.

The Club has long since disappeared from the Philadelphia scene, and with it have gone many wonderful memories of great people, great philatelists and great times.

* * *

Few, if any, reputable department stores will give you immediate credit for more than a nominal amount of merchandise without first making a thorough investigation. The same holds true in the stamp business.

When you send your first bid sheet or order to a stamp firm and enclose a list of your references, do not expect the dealer to immediately ship your merchandise on an open account. Unless the amount is quite small, the dealer will hold your purchase until his inquiries concerning your credit worthiness have been answered. Only after he has received the replies and found them satisfactory will he ship your material.

Credit investigations normally take from ten days to two weeks depending, of course, on where you live. In a large city like Philadelphia, such an investigation can usually be completed in a few hours or days simply by checking with the central credit bureau. However, if considerable correspondence over some distance is required, the investigation can drag on.

In all fairness to you and your dealer, when ordering from a new source, or bidding at an auction where you haven't previously purchased, submit your references and pay for your first purchase in advance of delivery if there hasn't been enough time for the proper inquiries to be made.

It is much easier for stamp dealers and auctioneers to ship in advance of payment, and they almost always will if they have the proper credit information. But, when for lack of information they bill in advance, cooperate with them and pay promptly. If the merchandise you purchased is not a represented they cheerfully refund your money.

* * *

Perhaps one of the saddest sights in stamp collecting is the man or woman who has for years collected only "new issues," that is, stamps as they are freshly available from dealers just after issue. While it is certainly true that, over a period of years, they may have acquired a large collection, they have missed one of the greatest thrills of philately—the search and find.

Most stamps are relatively easy to acquire. You decide what you want, write a check, and your favorite dealer furnishes the material. But it is those items which cannot be easily acquired that give stamp collecting its greatest allure. The items, without regard to price, which are so scarce and seldom seen that one must await their coming on the market—these are the true prizes of philately.

Those who limit their collecting to new issues never experience the pleasures of acquiring the difficult. And these collectors include many who would have made fine philatelists if only they had been aware of the great possibilities of philately.

* * *

The man was literally smothered in stamps—perhaps a million of them. Someday, he said, he would sell them all as a mail approval dealer. He admitted to being more than seventy years of age, and he hoped to get started within a year or two.

A survey of his stock revealed only common stamps that he had laboriously soaked from mixtures purchased on paper. Few of his stamps catalogued as much as twenty cents. Nevertheless, I wasn't one to disillusion this old gentleman. After much pleasant talk, I left him with a "good luck."

There is no satisfactory and profitable way to sell individual stamps such as this accumulation contained. Time, labor and selling expenses are all too costly for such merchandising. Material of this nature must be returned to mixture form. Then some collectors will buy it just to kill time and, perhaps, to catch an occasional "sleeper."

I'm afraid my elderly friend has already had his return from this stock in the pastime that soaking and sorting gave him. For that is all one may expect from a mixed lot of common stamps.

* * *

On several occasions, I have written about the effects of weather on stamps, particularly if they are stamps with gum on the back. In order to be properly preserved, these stamps should be stored in areas of low humidity and moderate temperature. So, too, must they be free of much weight or pressure.

Unfortunately, many collectors ignore these almost absolute rules. They believe that the use of "mounts" will free them of all other cares for their stamps. Or they believe that turning on an electric fan in the stamp closet on humid days will elminate the possibility of sticking and staining stamps. As much as we would hope so, all too often these well intentioned actions just don't furnish the needed protection. The bacteria that stain the stamps by ingesting the gum and excreting brown waste, thrive on moist warmth—in or out of mounts. Gum becomes tacky at temperatures that are normal in summer, particularly near the sea coast or in the south.

Continual air conditioning, placing albums vertically on shelves, and keeping them free of tightness, are the best methods of avoiding trouble. There are others, depending on your location, that will serve you well. If you live on an island in the Gulf of Mexico or some similar place, collect only used stamps because they are easier cared for than the unused o.g. variety.

If you have any love for your collection, the least you can do is preserve it in the best possible condition.

* * *

A collector in Savannah, Georgia presented me with his stamp collecting problem. He collects stamps of the British Empire and is willing to spend substantial amounts of money. He wanted to know why he was unable to receive satisfactory approval selections such as he had been able to get years ago when forming previous collections.

There must be many collectors that the stamp trade can no longer cater to as it did in the pre-1940 period. Labor costs, price competition, turn-over requirements and the potential losses of the approval business have relegated it to a sales form only suitable for juveniles and beginners. During the first stages of stamp buying, the matter of price and condition do not take on the importance they later acquire. Standard approval mailings can arouse interest and induce sales that aren't possible from more sophisticated collectors such as my Savannah friend.

* * *

It seems that novelists who aim to succeed in these times must shock their readers. The quality of the writing, the emotions aroused by the plot, and the message of the books, are nothing, unless the action takes place in the bedroom or back alley. Now quite a lot of stamp collecting is living off the same thing—shock.

The countries of the world are vying with one another in search of design, shape, color and topic that outdoes past exotic "stamp art." Frankly, I am amazed at the current circular, map shaped, 3, 4, 5 and 6-sided purple and gold splashes on paper, aluminum, etc., that now pass for postage stamps. And, perhaps like you, I am impatiently awaiting to see what comes next.

* * *

I have known perhaps 100,000 stamp collectors during a lifetime devoted to stamp dealing. These have included people of every grade of philatelic achievement from beginners to advanced specialists. Of them all, it is easy to select those who secured the most return from our hobby.

They are the ones who collected the stamps they liked best without regard for style, present popularity, potential increase in value, or what the other fellow was doing.

Stamp collecting, at its best, is a highly individualistic endeavor. The stamps you collect, the way you arrange them, whether you exhibit them or not, the matter of joining a club or not, are best decided on the basis of what you like.

Collect blocks or covers or precancels or anything else if it is your pleasure to do so. But if they bore you, or if the collection that gave you enthusiasm last year no longer excites you—remember philately is your relaxation.

* * *

From time to time someone asks me what I think of a new or recent issue of United States stamps. It amazes them to hear that I don't know anything about, or perhaps haven't seen the particular stamps in question.

This isn't because I lack curiosity about our latest issues. It isn't because I downgrade America's stamps, or because I depreciate the philatelic value of studying current issues. It's simply that the philatelic world is so vast, and the 250,000 or so past issues so numerous, that I seldom find time to watch the philatelic present.

The United States stamps issued after the Flag series of 1943 are more or less a blur to me. Perhaps it is because they lack scheme. They are mostly a mass of individual stamps, generally tied to a purpose or event that doesn't stand out in our history. We need sets of stamps distinctive in appearance and issued for important reasons.

Our earlier issues demonstrate what I mean. The Columbians, Pan Americans, Panama Pacifics, and others of that time are not all lookalikes. The range of their denominations make for varying degrees of scarcity. They didn't make every day a "new issue day" and dull the excitement of such events. They distinctively impressed themselves on stamp collectors.

I'm for a return to those stamp issuing principles.

* * *

What causes a boom in the price level of a country's stamps? I don't refer to the gradual, expected increase that takes place on a worldwide basis. I mean the San Marino and Vatican type of sudden price spurt that took place in the mid 1960's.

Sometimes, it is true, a long hidden condition of real scarcity is discovered and leads to the upward price rush. But more often, this price jump is the direct result of an intense promotion by interested principles.

A group of knowledgeable "professionals" can, by clever publicity and wash sales, popularize and greatly inflate the price of any philatelic issue. These "professionals" defend their actions by calling attention to the excitement they create within the hobby. This is good, they claim, because many collectors are held to stamps by their love of speculation—and this important segment of collectors is needed.

Perhaps they are right. I won't pass on their ethics or morality. But for me—and for the great majority of stamp lovers—the beauty, pleasure, education, and social qualities of stamp collecting will always be most exciting and most important.

* * *

On hundreds of occasions I have heard men of middle age lament the day they parted with their boyhood stamp collections. Their usual reason is that the collection would today be of great value.

Sometimes this is true, but most often the "kid" collections of thirty, forty or fifty years ago were nothing more than an accumulation of poor-conditioned common stamps. The exceptions were those cases in which an adult assisted in the formation of the collection, with both personal attention and money.

Just as it takes money to get the better stamps today, so it was in 1910, 1920, and 1930. Children of those days couldn't get very far toward building a valuable collection on their twenty-five or fifty cents a week spending money. All they could do was enjoy and learn from the general run of plentiful material. Millions did just that.

So don't mourn the loss of your beginning album. Use the knowledge that you have gained to build a truly fine collection in the part of your life that remains.

* * *

Despite all that has been written about the financially unsound venture of "new issue" collecting, there are still many thousands of people who are going to send their kids through college, retire, or make an enormous profit by purchasing sheets of United States stamps as issued from the post office and laying them away for years.

There is nothing wrong with "new issue" collecting, if you derive enjoyment from it. However, consider these facts if you are only interested in profit.

Since 1943 there have been over a thousand varieties issued by our country. At most, a dozen or two of these issues today sell for a slight premium over face value. If liquidating today, holders of stamps from this twenty-one year period must usually take a 10% to 20% loss from face value, depending on the denominations of their stamps.

If you are really seeking to send your kids through college on stamps, go to a good reliable dealer and buy old stamps in fine condition that have already become scarce and are presently bringing a good price. These stamps show a consistent increase in value year after year. Recent purchases from the U.S. Post Office are never going to become rare or even scarce during your lifetime.

When you must pay $5 for a stamp with a face value of 5 cents, it is already desirable and probably quite limited in supply. With the increase in population, the normal loss of stamps through mishandling, and the dispersal of the available supply, you may be sure that the stamp will sell for a higher price each year.

* * *

Any intelligent person will investigate the reliability of a lawyer, real estate agent, stock broke, jeweler or banker before dealing with him. It would be considered rash and senseless to spend large sums of money with a person of questionable reputation.

Yet, the same individual who is most careful about his ordinary business dealings will buy, without compunction, from "here today and gone tomorrow" stamp merchants. Without inquiring about the dealer's knowledge, resources or dependability, he will pay his money and take the dealer's word for genuineness, quality, condition, and the other factors that govern stamp value.

I have seen the result of such dealings many times when discussing the sale or auction of collections. It is most painful to tell a collector that certain of his prized stamps are counterfeit or of very poor quality.

In all businesses, you will find a small percentage of "shady" characters. Stamp dealing is no exception. My only advice is to use the same caution in buying stamps that you would use in purchasing diamonds, stocks or real estate. You'll be happier in the long run if you do.

* * *

I attend many stamp exhibitions each year, and I never fail to notice that only those local collectors who are already affiliated with organized philately manage to visit the shows.

These are the people who are already informed about the finer points of stamp collecting. The unaffiliated collectors, who far outnumber those in attendance and who can most benefit from the knowledge to be gained by viewing a good exhibition, rarely show up!

A stamp show in a western city recently recorded an outstanding turnout. Yet, despite attractive newspaper, radio and television publicity, eight unaffiliated stamp collectors of my acquaintance couldn't find time to see the excellent exhibition.

This just shouldn't happen. Philately is more than placing a hinge on a stamp and putting it in an album. Philately is a sharing of knowledge and ideas. No matter how much you may know about the hobby, you are sure to learn a little more by observing another philatelist's efforts, and perhaps another philatelist can learn something by observing your efforts as well.

You don't have to join a stamp club. There will always be a place in the hobby for "lone-wolf" collectors, but if the avocation of stamp collecting is good enough for you to be one of its followers, then it should be of sufficient worth for you to support it. One way to support philately is to be attending the local stamp shows.

* * *

Our friend and customer, Mr. R. T. has been a steady buyer every week since 1932. His visits are as regular as our store openings. His enthusiasm for stamps remains as keen today as it was when he started collecting. He collects stamps to enjoy, to learn, and to satisfy a natural inclination to accumulate and save something.

His acquisition of stamps isn't haphazard. It is a planned effort to gather in his albums material that completes certain geographical areas. In addition anything that is collateral to the stamps is welcome.

His continual buying over so long a period has resulted in a large and valuable collection, as he has never passed up an opportunity to acquire the scarce and better items needed for completion. I hope he will be able to go on enjoying stamps for many more years.

It is collectors such as R.T. who, when the time comes to reap a harvest from their philatelic sowing, are able to say: "I made a profit." The pleasure of the years compounded many times by the inner satisfaction of being a good philatelist when added to the recovery value at the end of his life collecting constitutes far more than bank interest.

* * *

There has never been a time when all the earth's people were peacefully satisfied with the status quo. Mankind's volatile condition is natural. Innovation, revolution, contest, construction and demolition constitute the ways in which mankind has progressed from caves to commonwealths.

These are the principles of every activity. The great natural migrations, the wars, the discoveries and inventions and even the changes in family life, are part of it.

Certainly philately cannot be contrary to everything else. It can and must change with time. The stamp collecting of 1904 was of a nature that satisfied collectors of that day. But this is a different era, one in which a greater knowledge of world affairs is involved with the fantastic production of attractive stamps in an excessive number. Collectors simply must draw limitations on their individual philatelic activities in an effort to remain collectors and still have time for other things in their lives.

Interest in the varied phases of philately continues, but because of their variety, it is fractionalized. No longer is it possible to assemble within the confines of a city, fifty or one hundred philatelists who collect in a similar way. Now each is pursuing a different course.

This is neither good nor bad. It is in line with the laws of life that decree eternal change. The lesson to be learned from this is that tomorrow will bring a still different philately. No one can forsee what it will be. Therefore no one should advise collectors to spend their money with investment in mind. The value of any certain stamps in the future is beyond our prophetic ability.

* * *

If you were to ask me to name the one event in my philatelic experience which had the most profound affect on stamp collecting activity in the United States, I would have to respond:"The affair of the Hammerskjold error."

This long, bitterly contested issue between the Postmaster and the hobby, created a volume of stamp collecting publicity far beyond any ever received—either before or since. And while tempers flared over the question of "Postmaster Day's decision," old appetites for collecting were whetted and revived.

Former collectors who hadn't looked into their albums in years suddenly became avid philatelists. Quite inadvertently, Postmaster Day had infused an interest in stamp collecting far beyond the reaches of stamp columns, Popular Mechanics advertisements and stamp society efforts.

I have never heard of Postmaster Day being selected for a philatelic honor of any sort, but in my book, he can very well be named: "Public Relations Philatelist of the Century".

* * *

Stamp collectors are frequently blinded by garish advertisements. Ads which offer merchandise with a $250 catalog value for only $17.50 attract a lot of attention and get many orders. However, most of these orders come from collectors who haven't learned to apply the rule of life that "you never get something for nothing" to their philatelic purchasing.

It stands to reason that merchandise of quality—whether in stamps, clothing, automobiles, real estate or any other line—doesn't have to be given away or sold at just a fraction of its worth.

If a stamp with a catalog value of $10.00 is so common or in such poor condition that it can only be sold for 50¢ or $1, then that is all the stamp is worth. It has evidently been overpriced in the catalog.

There will always be offerings of "much for little," and there will never be a shortage of takers of these offers, but when the time comes to put a true value on the material involved, there will always be a rude awakening.

* * *

If you are like most people I know, you find very little time to just sit and think. And, for many of us, there are quite a few things we would like to think about.

Our thinking doesn't have to be profound or transcendental. It isn't necessary for us to devise a new philosophy or solve some of life's great riddles. All we need to make our thinking worthwhile is the better understanding of one or more problems. Anything beyond that is pure cream.

But thinking isn't easy—especially at today's helter-skelter pace. One barely has time to react, much less think, and profitable thinking requires a composed mind.

What can we do? We can't rely on sedatives for they are hardly conducive to clear thinking, and we can't beat a retreat to Walden as Thoreau once did, but we can turn to our stamp albums.

There is nothing else known to man that so beneficially soothes the temper, the temperament, and the tedium. Stamp collecting is probably the greatest restraining influence on the sale of tranquilizers.

Use it when you want to just sit and think, and you'll be amazed at the results.

* * *

I was surprised when an old stamp collecting friend told me that he doesn't subscribe to a single stamp journal! He has been collecting stamps for over thirty years and has a large collection which he seems to enjoy. However, for some unknown reason, he has no interest in news of other collectors, collecting activities, discoveries, new issues or the myriad goings-on in the philatelic world.

I wonder if this particular collector is unique or if there are many like him. I also wonder if he—and his approach to the hobby—are symbolic of the people who form the collections that we and other dealers are never anxious to buy when they come up for sale.

We see thousands of these collections every year. They lack quality. They are completely devoid of interest of any sort. They are almost always poorly arranged, and to my mind, they are often downright worthless.

True, there is no fixed way to collect stamps, but no matter how you do it, you are bound to learn more about your hobby by reading the journals of philately and by joining other collectors in philatelic activities.

If you are going to discover all of stamp collecting by yourself, you will make costly errors. Of that, nothing can be more certain.

* * *

Ask your corner grocer—if you still have one—what mark-up he must place on slow-moving items that currently sell for ten cents or less. Then go to your local 5 & 10¢ store to see if there is such a thing as 5 & 10¢ merchandise. If you really want to spend an enlightening day, visit all the stores in your local shopping area seeking out items that sell for ten cents or less. The chances are you'll find mighty few of them, and the reason is simple; it isn't possible for a clerk to handle the receipt, checking, placing on sale and selling of such inexpensive goods in sufficient enough quantities to pay today's wages and the general overhead of even the best run businesses.

Yet there are thousands of stamp-collectors who expect to buy the inexpensive individual stamps required for their collections at a dime or less each—on special order! Granted, the stamps involved are common and pretty generally with no individual intrinsic value, but the supplier of the stamps has salaries and rent to pay—and his own time to account for.

Alas, I join with you in regretting the passing of the penny, nickel and dime stamp business, but so, too, do I regret the passing of the ten-cent shoe-shine.

* * *

One of my grandmothers came to the United States from Holland in 1853 when she was only two months of age. She was a very patriotic American. She proudly flew the flag on every occasion, and she showed-off Philadelphia's Liberty Bell to every out-of-town visitor.

Every American achievement was her pride and joy. Yet she never ceased to be concerned with what happened to her Dutch homeland. She feared for it in times of flood. During World War I she feared the Kaiser's invasion and the awesome blockades that made life so difficult.

Almost everyone feels a special attachment to the land of his or her ancestry. This sort of attachment has frequently resulted in stamp collectors' restricting their philatelic interests to the countries of their ancestors. Sometimes there is a familiarity with the language or customs that proves to be especially helpful to specialization.

It is most appropriate when a Greek collects stamps from Greece, or a Swede collects stamps from Sweden, etc. Not only is it appropriate, but the results are often an outstanding specialized collection that is a real credit to its maker.

There are many reasons for choosing a subject in which to specialize, but none is more worthy than the ties of ancestry.

* * *

We all know a few of the "I could have bought it" boys. They're the collectors who didn't have the foresight to buy items like U.S. Zeppelins, Wipa Sheets, Greek Olympics, etc., when they were low in price, and now they lament in public whenever they have the chance.

These collectors don't realize that everyone has, at some time or another, missed out on what later proved a bonanza. Perhaps it was a piece of real estate or a painting by a later recognized great artist, or, in the case of philately, the many stamps that time has determined were worth higher prices.

It is not what you didn't buy that really counts, it is what you did buy, and more important still, it is what you will buy from now on. There is no stamp collecting pleasure in lamentation. Look to the present and the future, not to the past. There will always be items which advance in price, and you are bound to have some of them if you continually add to your collection.

The important thing in stamp collecting is to get daily enjoyment from the hobby. With most collectors that enjoyment comes from the items they are continually adding to their collections—even if some of them do fail to become rarities.

* * *

It may be difficult for you to imagine the many thousands of earnest stamp collectors for whom no stamps exist outside of the communist area, or from before the communist take-over of their country. But there is such a group of collectors in Czechoslovakia.

The government of that communist satellite sees to it that no foreign catalogs, stamps or even information about issues from the west is available. Perhaps one of the reasons for the multiplicity of issues from iron and bamboo curtain countries is to give collectors a wide range of material to keep them interested in their restricted hobby.

In the free countries of the world, there is a continual striving for all kinds of knowledge. In the communist countries, people can only strive for the knowledge that their government wants them to have.

The collectors in these countries, as individuals, are just as pleasant and friendly as our own hobbyists. It is too bad that they can only buy, sell and collect on a restricted basis which most of us would find detestable.

* * *

The house and its furnishings indicated a degree of poverty. The nice lady and gentleman who lived there were seeking my advice. It seemed that he couldn't work because of a crippling illness. She held a modest position. What did I think of them putting as much as they could, perhaps twenty dollars a month, into stamps so that when she goes on social security in fifteen years, they would have a nest egg of considerable value.

I hesitate to give advice that should be sought from other professions. In this case, a banker or broker was needed. I hope that I was able to persuade these misguided folks to seek out a good bank and be happy with its savings plans.

There is a cost level at which everyone can afford stamp collecting. It may be even as low as one dollar a month. However, there has never been a time when small money is likely to be the entry way to philatelic riches. The pleasures of stamp collecting are for everyone. Its financial returns are for the few with the knowledge and capital required for what is perhaps the trickiest of investments.

People with only five dollars a week and the need of future savings had better put a least four dollars in a bank, and collect stamps modestly for the remaining dollar. We hope they will expect their return to be entirely in pleasure.

* * *

Some people are obsessed with what for want of a better term can be called "counterfititis." They have gotten into such a frame of mind that they believe it their duty to prove that every stamp is either a fake or has been tampered with.

Now in truth, only a very small percentage of philatelic material is the product of counterfeiters or repairers, and almost all of their work is readily recognized by experienced professionals. It is doubtful if one tenth of one percent of the efforts of fakers could get by the describers employed by the leading stamp businesses of the world.

When there is real reason for doubt, every stamp firm urges the submission of material to one of the many fine recognized expert committees for an opinion. If the opinion is negative, I know of no established stamp dealer who won't make good—of course within the limits of his sales guarantee which is always generous enough to allow plenty of time for having your purchases checked. There probably is no other line of business that is so ethical in this respect as is the stamp trade.

* * *

Suppose you were the postmaster general of a small country. You received an annual salary equivalent to about $8,000 or $10,000 per year. Suppose too, that your august position required private schools for your children, maintaining a fine home, entertaining on a lavish scale, and all the other burdens of prominence.

Unless you were independently wealthy with outside sources of income, isn't it possible that you might be susceptible to promoters of controlled stamp issues who offered you an "honest" way to increase your income by a few thousand dollars a year?

Some of the flood of "new issues" is unquestionably a result of connivances which situations such as the above engender. I don't think that this can be stopped at its source, but I do think that it would become far less profitable for its perpetrators if more American collectors used a little will power and rejected materials which the philatelic press has exposed as contrived rubbish.

Perhaps, as Mr. Barnum once pointed out, "there is a sucker born every minute." Do you have to be one of them?

* * *

Any stamp dealer worthy of patronage should know more about the stamps he sells than the average collector. Granted, unless he is a specialist in a particular field, he will seldom know as much as specialists do about the restricted sections of philately which they so intensely study.

What this means to you, the stamp collector who is buying for his collection, is that you should be able to buy with every confidence from your dealer. You should not have to worry about the more obvious fakes, repairs and misleading items that turn up. These should have already been eliminated from the merchandise which your dealer is offering.

Specialists with knowledge gained from concentrated study and research will always have an advantage over general dealers and collectors. These specialists will know and recognize varieties which are regularly offered for major numbers in most places. They have learned the "good" postmarks, the points that genuine stamps must bear, the required postal rates of covers, and much other information that would sorely over-burden any individual if he tried to learn all about everything. General dealers should know some of this, but can never know all.

Specialists are frequently repaid for their intensive studies by the opportunities they get for picking up "sleepers." But they must often invest a great deal more time in study than they are repaid in the "good buys" they make.

Only a small percentage of stamp collectors are inclined to be studious specialists. For the rest of us, the general world of stamps is our fascination. If a broken "T" exists in position 23 of plate 16 of the $10.00 denomination of the 1938 issue of Yemen, that knowledge, so precious to a few, is of little import to the great body of our hobby.

* * *

While on a buying tour through Florida during October and November, I conversed with well over one-hundred collectors. All except a dozen or so insisted that the precautions necessary to protect against the gum and stamp damage caused by a hot humid climate did not apply to them.

I heard such inane statements as: "I keep my stamps in a dry closet," and "I use mounts on all my stamps". From where I'm sitting, it seems obvious that without climate control of some sort, humidity will get into a closet just as easily as it gets into a closed-up basement or attic. And mounts have never been known to protect gum that is softened by high temperature and dampness.

The only sure-fire protection for unused stamps in hot, humid areas is a well regulated air conditioning system. This is a very low cost investment in comparison to the value of most collections, and if limited to only one room in a house, the investment in climate control is practically nil.

There is never any justifiable reason for anyone losing a collection by not caring for it. That is, there is no reason other than the one of being blind to the experiences of thousands of other collectors.

* * *

Nowadays, eveyone wants to get into everyone else's act. The chain stores are selling gasoline and the gasoline stations are selling general merchandise. The football season erupts in violent bloom long before baseball is even nearing its World Series. Coin shows are being run in competition with stamp exhibitions—sometimes even in the same hotel.

Few of us have enough leisure—or concentration—to be both football and baseball fans at one and the same time. Most men are limited by their budgets and must choose either stamp or coin collecting as a hobby, but certainly not both.

Joe, the gas station man, who was just breaking even before XYZ markets put in gas, oil and tires, now has another problem. Life and earning a living are becoming constantly more complex. Most individuals today are faced with tougher problems than their fathers could have imagined in their wildest dreams. What our opinion-makers refer to as "progress" is frequently just a bigger headache. Perhaps it is time to investigate the importance of personal contentment, peace of mind and enjoyment of life. They could deserve as much publicity as so-called "progress."

* * *

Ladies and Gentlemen! On your left is Mr. Topical Collector, and on your right, Mr. Conventional Philatelist. The fight is a "no holds barred" to the finish, to decide how stamps should be collected.

The above is the way some extremists would have the stamp collecting world view the differences in styles of our hobby. They are intolerant of variation from the "by country," "by date," and "by issue" form, or, if they are followers of thematics, cannot bear to accord rights to anything but that gathered by subject or event.

Every human endeavor including religion, politics, philosophy, and medicine has its share of rabid and intolerantly biased followers. They do little good and frequently do harm. We don't need them in philately. Much can be said for any form of collecting. If we exclude from our hobby, because of the plan they follow, any segment of stamp collectors, we are decreasing the market for stamps, and thus affecting the price level that is sensitive to all matters of supply and demand. We are also, and probably most harmfully, restricting the number of people who enjoy the pleasures and benefits of stamp collecting.

* * *

Many people miss the major reason for being a stamp collector. This occurs because they are misled by some factions of the philatelic press into believing that monetary gain is the main reason for the followers of philately to be addicted to the hobby.

Stamp collecting is basically an exciting diversion because it stirs the interests and emotions of its followers. It does this in various ways, but always in a constructive direction. Some collectors are urged by the hobby to seek certain stamps. They become quite emotional about looking for and getting the items they want.

Other collectors diligently seek the information they desire about the stamps they own. To them the plate positions or the types of postmark are as thrilling as a horse race or close ball game.

There are of course other exciting aspects of stamp collecting, even including stamp club membership and the way the club is conducted.

The dollar sign is an important one in our hobby, but without a stirring of the emotions, without the excitement of acquiring that piece that was difficult to find, without the pleasures of exhibiting to our fellow philatelists, stamp collecting would fall flat. Because our hobby offers these basic joys we are willing to spend varying amounts of money to pursue it. Few of us would be interested if the money value was philately's sole attraction.

* * *

Catalog value is often a misleading quotation when it is used to value collections for tax or probate purposes. The government appraiser who figures every 10¢ catalog item, who disregards condition, and to whom the popularity and current market are unknown, is in a poor position to place a value on stamps. Equally unqualified is the novice collector who, though he can read the catalog, has little experience in converting its figures into a fair resale price.

I have, during the past three months, come upon cases where tax was paid on an estate based on the full catalog value of common and poor quality stamps because the appraiser and the lawyer for the estate knew no better. Accurate appraisal of stamps requires years of experience. Estimating the worth of scarce varieties and unusual pieces is well beyond the ability of 99 out of 100 collectors. It is completely over the head of such appraisers as real estate men, numismatists, butchers, and haberdashers. I have seen the results achieved by these people, thoroughly competent in the above occupations, when they endeavored to value stamps. The hundreds of dollars in excess taxes paid by the estates they misvalued could well have gone to a worthy charity or toward making the widow's later years more comfortable.

* * *

The description "o.g." in stamp collecting means original gum as added to the stamp before its sale in the post office. Some new collectors are alarmed at the use of hinges to mount stamps in albums as has been done for over 100 years by collectors everywhere. They mistakenly believe that this best of all ways to mount stamps is injurious to the stamp.

Well, if the backs of stamps are the side to be displayed it must be admitted that hinges generally do make a mark on gum. But the gum is still original even though it shows that it has been hinged.

Gum may be (and frequently is) replaced or altered by those who seek to freshen up their stamps. If the job is well done even experts cannot tell the difference. So, I'd rather have a lightly hinged stamp, if it's over thirty years old, than a "never hinged" one, because there is a chance that the never hinged stamp is the possessor of gum that never saw the inside of a post office.

Paying through the nose for "mint"—and that is what the gum fanatics are doing in their mania for never hinged— and then getting gum that was in a bottle a short while before, strikes me as an even wilder way to squander money than going to the races.

This piece isn't likely to convert the "gum collectors," but at least it reiterates the basic rule that o.g. must not be construed as meaning never hinged. It's a more honest statement of condition than many "never hinged" stamps could ever claim.

* * *

Where can I get it? We are asked this question several times a day by collectors who seek certain elusive stamps which they would like to add to their collections. Sometimes, even though the catalog price is low, it takes years to locate some particular stamps. This shouldn't dismay the one who seeks them, because the difficulties of stamp collecting are responsible for its popularity with most collectors.

If all one needed was money to acquire every philatelic item desired, people of means would have a great advantage over the myriad of less affluent collectors. However, one soon learns that in philately there are some things money can't buy, and one of them is completeness. There is always the elusive item that no one has for sale, and for which one must wait until a great collection is being broken up. It is acquired only after years of patience.

I believe this aspect of our hobby is the one that keeps learned and cultured collectors in the fold. They seldom like projects that are easily completed.

* * *

In the last two months I have traveled over 30,000 miles in North and South America. I have seen the sights and scenery; I have tried the foods along the way, and I have slept in a myriad of different beds. I have met many stamp collectors and dealers. The courtesy and hospitality of our fellow philatelists is outstanding.

In Santiago, Chile; Montevideo, Uruguay; Rio de Janeiro, and San Paulo, Brazil; Buenos Aires, and San Carlos de Bariloche, Argentina; as well as Miami, St. Petersburg, Oakland, San Diego, and a hundred other places stamp collectors considered it a pleasure to go out of their way to make our visit enjoyable.

Some of these folks we had known through correspondence, but the majority of them were strangers until our visit. The fraternity of philately is a door opener and a lodge of true brothers.

The next time you travel look up a few collectors. You will agree that meeting with them constitutes one of our hobby's greatest pleasures.

* * *

For some difficult to discern reason there are in the United States uninformed speculators who seek to be duped. They have heard of the value of some stamps and, therefore, assume that all stamps are desirable and sell for ever increasing prices. Thus, when a fast talker offers them 50 sets of an issue from a country they never heard of at double or triple what it is available for from established dealers, they grab at the opportunity of a lifetime.

These speculators seldom even have a catalog, subscribe to magazines, and perhaps limit their philatelic reading to the stamp column appearing once a week in their local newspaper. An exhibition of stamps or an informative talk at the local club would not attract them because they believe that all one must know about stamps to be a successful speculator is how to write checks paying for them.

While it is true that these people are of no consequence to the established stamp trade, sooner or later they receive a grand disillusionment and then widely proclaim that stamp collecting is a fraud. How they should know is beyond me, since they never were stamp collectors.

* * *

Early in his stamp collecting experience it becomes evident to almost every collector that common sense is as applicable to the pursuit of his hobby as it is to all other activities.

He realizes that moderation is a necessity if he is to enjoy philately through the coming years. He must limit the time for, and cost of the hobby to the amount that his station in life affords. He must select from the thousands of forms of collecting, those that suit his personality, temperament and abilities. He must decide on the important matter of club association or lone wolf collecting. He must consider such obvious details as type of album, type of mounting, used or unused or both, along with the level of quality desired.

Good common sense will decide all these matters so that future years will provide a period of tranquil enjoyment of stamp collecting. As an aid may I suggest that the tried methods that developed with our grandfather's collections are still a path to philatelic enjoyment. Essentially they are to collect on a broad enough scale to maintain your interest; to seek ever to improve the quality of your specimens; to arrange your material as soon as possible in albums (envelopes, file drawers and cigar boxes are poor display accessories); to subscribe to, read and learn from several good stamp journals; to lend a helping hand to the novice collector so that he may benefit from your experience.

* * *

Where stamp collectors gather, be it in the club or the dealer's shop, there should be a sign reading, "Philately Spoken Here." Truly a distinctive language embracing a terminology that would be as Hottentot to most, but is used and understood internationally by philatelists. The references to catalogs and handbooks that we make so casually; the use of quality terms; the ways in which we divide shades, papers, perforations, postmarks and printing methods, are no secret to any of us, but constitute a rigid barrier to outsiders.

One can travel in any country of the world and speak "Philately" in stamp gatherings and be sure of a great degree of understanding by his audience. The same person cannot visit his next door neighbor and be understood when he talks in the stamp collecting language. We should bear this in mind when we address audiences of non-collectors or speak in groups where our hobby is not familiar.

We may use the language of philately only in philatelic circles. All others require interpretation in order to understand completely our message.

* * *

The philatelic gum collectors are very well entitled to their form of collecting; after all, no one in the stamp collecting world has laid greater emphasis on the right to collect what you choose than I have. If a collector desires stamps hinged only once or never hinged that is his privilege, and most stamp dealers will honor his wishes. He is not a problem when he carefully indicates his requirements.

On the other hand, there is a large group of people who, perhaps thoughtlessly, order stamps from lists or auction catalogs wherein condition is definitely described and defined, but either refuse to take the time to read the definitions before ordering, or hopefully chance getting material with qualities different than described.

The majority of stamp dealers secure their stock of all but current issues through the purchase of stamp collections. It was, and still is the custom of millions of collectors to use stamp hinges. When properly used good hinges do not, and I emphasize the "do not," harm stamps. It is virtually impossible to make a collection of any kind of unused stamps issued prior to 1940 and achieve completion unless previously hinged stamps are acceptable. The only alternative is to spend a lot of money buying stamps that have been regummed to mislead the great number of people who cannot tell original from regummed stamps.

The purpose of this editorial is twofold. First, to ask that you please do not mislead your dealer by ordering in such a way that he is unaware of your requirements, and, two, that you give reasonable thought to the matter of whether the stamp or its glue is what you are collecting.

* * *

Stamp shows, exhibitions, conventions and get-to-gethers are desirable and usually enjoyable. However, this is not reason enough for having the many thousands that are held yearly in the United States. One follows another frequently in the same area. The collections on exhibit are the same collections that go on the prize hunting circuit. And often, attendance is the same show-going crowd never large enough for the effort expended.

There are not enough fresh ideas, exhibitors, and show goers to sustain our present schedule successfully. There is no need for Central, North, East, South and West Middletown to each have its own exhibition and banquet. Yet this is what goes on in hundreds of cities.

A merging of interests into at least state wide groups is the answer. We travel today at high speed so that even in a state as wide as Montana those who are interested can and will attend a really worthwhile convention and exhibition at the far end of the state. They will not attend twenty different smaller shows on twenty week-ends as so often happens now. This calls for a merging of interest and joining together in our projects. The result must be an advantageous one.

* * *

The other night my wife and I attended the wedding of my secretary. She married a fine, brilliant young physicist whose future seems destined to be highly successful. The wedding party was in the main made up of young, attractive, well educated people striving for important places in America's expanding future.

In contrast, there were a few of the "older generation,"—those whose ultimate future has arrived and who are living now at the pinnacle of their achievement. For the most part, they grew up during a time when education wasn't the all and everything of youth. School ended for those born early in this century when economic pressure on the family overbalanced the scale of wonderment and curiosity that leads to higher education. College degrees were for the one in twenty-five or so who were touched by providential guidance. America today is the land of the young. The young number among them a greater percentage of well-educated, thinking, sophisticates than any generation in history. Stamp collecting in its most advanced forms is a pursuit extremely enjoyable to this great class of learned people. Considering the number of them in our new society, can you doubt that we are at the threshhold of philately's greatest expansion; that fine and scarce stamps have today only a fraction of the worth they will have before the end of this century; and that the cultural qualities of stamp collecting will be a part of many more in the future than it has been in the past.

* * *

It was a lazy rainy Sunday. I didn't even shave. Along about one o'clock in the afternoon I opened the door to our store-room with nothing more in mind than killing time. Within ten minutes I was completely absorbed looking over envelopes and album pages of stamps acquired years ago. Even one as close to stamp values as I am gets a pleasant surprise at finding fifty or a hundred stamps that were common and worth pennies when last looked at, and now catalog a dollar or more. Yet any older accumulator is able to get this pleasure. The market changes and ordinary stamps of the 1930 period are no longer current. To the present generation, stamps that were disdained thirty years ago are now quite desirable.

It has ever been this way in stamp collecting. The attrition of years of handling, economic change and increase of interest will, as it has in the past, continue to raise the price level of good stamps. Making a "find" in one's own closet happens quite often to collectors.

Taking care of your duplicates and accumulations is good business. The gains that can result over the years are truly amazing.

* * *

The pleasures of the past can be relived. I have just finished reading the series of stamp columns which I wrote for a newspaper syndicate in 1956 and 1957. They are many years old, and I had completely forgotten about them. The general philatelic topics of the series are as fresh today as they were then. In fact, I could use any of them for this column and readers would believe they were freshly written for just this one purpose.

This only goes to prove that most of what is exciting to the new collector has been repeated time and again during the more than a century of stamp collecting history. New issues, errors, record prices, famous collectors, exhibitions, scarcity of material, stamp thefts, conventions, etc.—they all happened before and gave those collectors the same reactions that we get today's happenings.

It is indeed a credit to the appeal and qualities of philately that the same acts and dramas can be repeated time and again to the joy of an ever increasing following. Your great-grandfather could barely await the weekly stamp club meeting back in 1901 so he could show his friends his latest find, an inverted One-cent Pan American. Now, many years later, Junior rushes to the meeting to participate in a current discussion about the lack of art in the stamps our country is currently issuing. The subject of Post Office delinquency is as hot today as it was in 1901. Philately is quite safe as long as this interest continues.

* * *

When the new *Scott Catalogs* are released, many collectors immediately check each price against the preceeding year's figure and determine the gain or loss for the year. Since in the majority of cases this is done with considerable enjoyment it becomes a part of the collector's philosophy of philatelic pleasure. Let him long continue to do everything that he likes to do in stamp collecting.

My purpose here is to call attention to the ever decreasing meaning of catalog value. It has been replaced by actual selling prices as given in the priced lists and catalogs of the more important dealers who both stock and sell stamps. Individual and unique rarities are priced at what the market will bear, often by sale at auction. The catalog can only hint at what will be paid for a distinctively fine gem that is not apt to be available again within the lifetime of interested buyers.

On the other hand, the great mass of stamps are available from stocks in the hands of professionals. With today's emphasis on condition prices are based more on that factor than on the general supply available, for, with the exception of recent stamps, time, handling, climate, and other hazards have taken a toll of many existing specimens.

A dealer offering the U.S. Columbian issues at $1/2$ Scott would only be able to supply stamps below the condition requirements of most buyers. It, therefore, has become necessary for him to ignore catalog price and establish his net retail price on a basis of cost to him, realized prices at recent auctions, probable sources and cost of replacement and projected future market. Since you buy from him but not from Scott, his price must ultimately receive more consideration than catalog price.

* * *

What is the right price for a stamp? Is a particular specimen worth two or three, or even more times the catalog value while another is no bargain at a sixth or a seventh of Scott? Every collector at one time or another must consider these questions. If he tries to decide without the benefit of experience and knowledge, he is apt to be a patsy for those who make a business of finding stamp collecting patsys.

It is necessary to devote some of your stamp collecting time to learning about stamps from authoritative literature and periodicals. An enormous amount of worthwhile information is available to every collector. If you live thousands of miles from a philatelic library, you can, for a modest expenditure, form your own reference library. The stamp trade has for sale fine books on almost every subject in philately that you can imagine.

The best way to know if you are getting your money's worth in stamp collecting is to spend a little of that money learning about your subject.

There is a society, The American Philatelic Society, that among other things publishes frequent journals reviewing new publications and offering worthwhile books. Dues are modest per year, and to become a member, simply write for information to Box 8000, State College, PA 16801. Send in your application today and take advantage of the unlimited knowledge available through this society.

* * *

I have no objection to a little stretching of the truth when it results in improving an anecdote or increases the humor of a situation. It is human nature to embellish upon the truth, and topping the next fellow seems to be enjoyable in all circumstances.

However, there is one situation where honesty and accuracy is desirable. That is in informing your family of the real worth and finances of your collection. Misleading the Missus in either the direction of undervaluing or overvaluing your stamp holdings can lead to some real heartache if she ever must supervise their disposal. Telling her that you have been the world's best buyer of stamps won't hold up under those circumstances. On the other hand, making her believe that you spend little or nothing on the hobby when, in truth you put into it all but the baby's shoe money is just as bad.

Every man is entitled to a fund, within reason, for his pleasure. Take your wife into your confidence and insist that she know what your collection is worth, and what to do with it if something happens to you. You may be saving her considerable heartache in the long run by such frank action now.

* * *

Again and again we are faced with the necessity of telling widows or other heirs that the collection they have inherited has only the value of the pleasure it has given its maker.

The assemblage of common stamps, scattered incomplete sets, mixed used and unused, ordinary covers, and kindred material that many collectors form can only be for the joy of so doing. It is true that a high total of catalog value can be accumulated in this way. It certainly can be costly if the material is acquired stamp by stamp at top price for each item, but the end result is a collection that duplicates millions of others and one in which an informed philatelist will find no single item of rarity or high value.

Collections of this sort are sold on the basis of the wholesale value of a packet of comparable size.

All advanced collectors started out making such a collection. Then they wrote off most of the cost to pleasure and education received from elementary general collecting.

The further advanced a collector becomes, the higher the percentage of recovery of his costs, provided that he adds both quality and scarcity to his collection. Beginning efforts that may carry on for years are certain to be full of mistakes. Only those who learn from their mistakes and go on to more knowledgeable stamp collecting are the ones who may make a gain from collecting.

* * *

I have concluded that lack of system accounts for many dealers failing in the stamp business. They buy at favorable prices and sell fairly. They do all the right things except keep stock in a methodical and merchandiseable manner.

The easy but unsatisfactory method of using glassine envelopes or stock books as a place to hide stamps of all qualities eventually is costly. Used or unused, very fine and just good, blocks and singles, etc., don't all belong in one envelope or on one stock page. When you are beginning and the stock is small you might remember where everything is, but you soon outgrow such status.

Time spent going through fifty stamps to find one is time lost. Sales lost because you don't know what you have are not replaceable. Yet, there are far more dealers and accumulators with "shoe box" stocks than dealers with well arranged, ready-for-sale material.

And then when the "reaper" calls to end it all, appraisers and buyers are expected to take the time needed to burrow through the endless loose and ill sorted accumulations, looking for the value that might be there. It was too much effort for the owner to keep things straight, but the friendly buyer from the big city should do free, the job the owner never did for myself.

If you are carelessly piling up stamps faster than you can arrange them, call a halt until you catch up. Sort by quality. Sort by used and unused. Keep things in order and you will be one of those who succeed. Otherwise, the chance of failure is high.

* * *

One of the difficulties faced by today's stamp clubs is the problem of arranging programs with a broad enough base of interest to hold the attention of a large group of collectors. In recent years, the fragmentation of philately has resulted in collectors who restrict their activities to smaller, more manageable collecting areas. Some restrict their activities to even so small a field as collecting only one stamp and its varieties. Years ago everyone collected everything.

There is no doubt that the answer to this problem is difficult to find. For clubs that meet weekly, the arranging of 52 attractive programs each year constitutes a large sized headache.

There are, in the United States, several clubs that have for many years been meeting weekly and enjoying a large and interested attendance. They are well known and they prosper in such cities as Cleveland; Portland, Oregon; Los Angeles; Seattle; and Chicago.

It would be a service to philately if the programs of some of these clubs as offered over a period of a year could be publicized. It would result in other clubs getting some ideas for their own meetings. I suggest a series of articles each on a different club telling just what their activities were for an entire year. These articles might just furnish the stimulus needed by dozens of stamp groups around the country to spark a renaissance of stamp club activity.

* * *

In 1966, in a burst of publicity, the final closedown of a forger and counterfeiter who lived in Merida, Mexico was disclosed. I wish to express my personal appreciation for the part played by various American Philatelic society officers and members in this drama.

May I say that the dishonest dealings of Raoul De Thuin were known of for many years to the American stamp trade. The fact that he sold "rarities" of his own make at great discounts was no secret anywhere. That collectors throughout the world were credulous enough to believe that a stamp dealer located in a remote province of Mexico could continually have such "rarities," and be foolish enough to sell them at fractions of what they would bring in the great philatelic markets, is a sad reflection on the judgement used by many in purchasing stamps for their collections.

Undoubtedly, through resale of collections, much of this privately manufactured material has been redistributed and now reposes in collections and stocks where it isn't recognized for what it is in truth—just junk, even though the A.P.S. published its book enabling us to recognize these forgeries, some found with regret that believed treasures were worthless. This should result in eveyone using greater care in the future.

Questioning the genuineness of rare overprints until they are proved otherwise, is reasonably good sense. The money spent to buy good philatelic literature and learn what is what, should be considered a necessary expense of collecting; and above all, when you are offered stamps at prices far below their normal market value, do more than raise your eyebrows. Knowledgeable dealers don't "give away" rarities. Buying from dealers who aren't knowledgeable, sooner or later, results in many regrets.

* * *

I recently took a 26-day cruise. There were 117 passengers on the ship. So far as I could determine, none of them collected stamps. Many of them had collecting friends for whom they bought assortments and packets at the various ports where we stopped. Almost all my fellow passengers were between 50 and 70 years of age, well-to-do—and they invariably complained of leading boring lives. Isn't it deplorable that they had not been ensnared by one of the better collecting hobbies earlier in life—one that now, when they have the leisure and the means to enjoy it, would carry them through the dull, uninteresting hours of later life?

The time to prepare for leisure is when you don't have it. The time to know the joy of a suitable diversion is now, so that you can carry it with you into the "later on,"when its need is greatest. The wise man will, in his youth, stake out guide lines for the years to come and place his guide lights at the broad intervals that will make the doing of likable things a part of his plans.

* * *

There is a great deal of misleading information in much of stamp collecting publicity. To my mind, the very worst publicity from the viewpoint of recruiting new collectors is the overemphasis of the sale of great rarities for high prices. It frightens off innumerable potential philatelists. They get the impression that only millionaires can make fine collections.

Every reader of these articles knows how untrue this is. They know that for each collector who can afford thousand-dollar rarities there are a thousand people of average income following our hobby and enjoying it fully. As a matter of fact, not one collector in a thousand ever pays as much as one hundred dollars for an individual addition to his collection.

There are dozens or even hundreds of forms of stamp collecting that can be followed for an entire lifetime and not demand the acquisition of costly stamps. So let us make known the possibilities of our hobby for the man who occasionally has to hurry to the bank to cover his checks. Let us stop scaring him away. And, while we are at it, why not introduce a new classification into local stamp shows of exhibits in which no single item costs the owner over ten dollars.

Lest all this be misunderstood, my firm sells many rarities and has in stock at all times valuable and expensive material—but we recognize that philately is an avocation suitable to all and that most of us are not wealthy. We appeal for common sense public relations that will not deter many of the prospective recruits from the pleasures of collecting.

* * *

We are all aware of the great breadth of interest in stamp collecting. We will realize that it can entertain even the most erudite as well as those of just ordinary learning and intelligence. It not only entertains them but also adds to their knowledge and frequently is the mental tonic so badly needed in these days of taut tensions and frayed nerves.

But how many of us know that this self-same hobby of ours is also a useful and important part of the curriculum in schools for special needs people? True, the collections these folks usually form will not be exhibitable in select philatelic circles; nor will anyone be likely to point to them as being outstanding in the usual ways we judge collections. They are, however, a means of interesting those with relatively low intelligence to recognize beauty, form and arrangement, and to add some knowledge of history and geography to an otherwise meager background.

Stamp collecting, to be helpful to those with special needs, should have the guidance from an informed collector or teacher who recognizes the motivation possible in philately. If you can spare the time you will no doubt be welcomed by your local special needs children's association to aid in this facet of their education.

* * *

Many thousands of collectors have never purchased any stamps except as new issues. While I cannot quite understand the pleasure derived from such easy stamp collecting, it is their privilege to collect as they will. On the other hand, every one of them is missing the joy of the hunt, the thrill of the acquisition and the elation of accomplishment that are part of building a collection of earlier issues. You don't send an order to an agency or a single dealer for a complete collection of Peru or Andorra. You cannot get all the purple stamps of the world by walking into a store and requesting them. Neither can you understand the 19th century history of Europe quite as well as the collector who carefully and enjoyably, over a period of time, assembles a representative collection of European stamps issued during those years.

And, most surprisingly, it costs less money to collect the older stamps than the current flood of emissions. A budget that can accommodate all the new issues of the world could within a few years afford a Grand Award-winning collection of an unlimited number of stamp groups. Of course it would require some study, some searching and some patience, but then the end result of having really accomplished a philatelic challenge is exhilarating enough to most of us to more than repay the extra effort.

Last but by no means least, I have yet to see a fine collection of older material that lacks a market at all times, good or bad. This cannot always be said about collections formed only of new issues.

* * *

A correspondent has written to me complaining that my references to First Day Covers are not praiseworthy enough. He objects to my calling them sideline philatelic material. I believe that his objection is based on a lack of understanding of stamp collecting. Actually everything that we put into our collection is "sideline" except the stamps.

The most important part of philately has always been, is, and will be stamp collecting. When we elaborate on this by adding covers, margin markings, essays, proofs, pertinent documents, autographs and what not, we are constructively adding to the interest and value of our hobby. I am heartily in favor of all the things that I referred to as sidelines, and my firm does considerable business in each of them.

Still, if we use reason, we realize that the value of every sideline exists only because we are primarily stamp collectors.

* * *

Most of us are moody. We feel exuberant on Monday and Tuesday. Then something happens that we don't like, and all day Wednesday we act as if the end of the world would be most welcome. We are up and down in greater or lesser degree for what are generally trivial reasons.

Stamp collecting suffers its ups and downs in the same way. We go great guns on the albums for a period of time. Then, perhaps for no more important a reason than the visit of a disliked relative or the receipt of a thinned stamp in a long set, we are cold to our hobby for a while.

All this seems to be the nature of man. It extends to everything he does. The salesman has his good and bad days even while calling on the same prospects. The research scientist bungles as much as he succeeds. The ball player must have his slumps and his phenomenal streaks.

If stamp collecting leaves you a little cold this week, don't despair. Next week or next month it will again be the greatest.

* * *

During more than forty-five years of membership in and contact with philatelic organizations, I have found them to be almost completely free of the bigotries and antagonisms that so frequently enter into other phases of life. In my personal experience, a man's ancestry, faith or race have seldom been asked when he applied for stamp club membership.

The international viewpoint that is fostered by stamp collecting may in part be responsible for the general broad-mindedness of its followers. One will certainly gain appreciation of all peoples by contact with them, and stamps are the finest armchair method of acquiring each contact. It isn't likely that anyone familiar with the art, history and great people of a country as portrayed by its stamps will think of those descended from that country as being less than equal to all others.

The followers of any religious faith can only be struck by the similarities of all religions as he studies stamps of religious significance.

The races of mankind join in a stamp album to form a club that is vast in learning, mutually helpful for scientific and cultural progress and, despite differences of appearance, includes all the children of the same scheme of nature.

It is very unlikely that prejudice will ever be a barrier to a philatelic association. Our basic item, the postage stamp, is far too cosmopolitan to permit it.

* * *

Take a look at the advertisements of stamp dealers. Did you ever notice how few of them stay in the business for as long as five years? Many of the big advertisers of 1960 have long since gone. The new ones in their place will mostly peter out by 1990.

This is a tough business. Along with sharp competition we are faced with the everpresent need of fresh stock that cannot be ordered from a factory. The WIPA sheet that our customer wants isn't waiting in a warehouse for our order.

Then there are the expensive handling costs of the lower-priced stamps which are a necessary part of a collection and should be available in our stock for our clients.

To cap it off, style trends are endless. The singles collector becomes a block collector just after you have broken up your block stock to have singles for sale. And so it goes. Still, of all the businesses I know, this is the one I prefer. I like the smile of our satisfied clients and I like to greet the number of them we have served for four generations.

* * *

In fifty years of philatelic activity it has always been my experience that France is one of the most popular countries. Through good and bad times, war and peace, the land of the Gauls has issued much sought after philatelic material. Of course, the home market in France itself is a strong factor in this popularity; but overseas in the former colonies, in Latin America, in French Canada, and throughout Europe, quality stamps of France always enjoy a strong market.

Recent issues of French stamps are artistic gems. Many early issues are classics of considerable value, and the so-called middle issues lend themselves to minor specialization at modest cost. There are many albums and catalogs available to aid the collector. This is one country that appears to have a feel for the collector as strong as *he* has for its stamps.

* * *

It is just possible that American collectors can do something about the lagging market in recent United States stamps. A campaign of protest to the Postmaster General against the continuing issuance of one denomination commemoratives, each in enormous quantities, might call his attention to the need for change—change to sets of stamps with a variety of denominations, each issued in a different quantity. The demand for 75¢ or $1.25 stamps is a fraction of that for the 20¢ value. Thus, we might once again restore to the stamps of our country some issues that might have more than postage value to stamp collectors.

Another advantage to sets is that a range of subjects pertaining to the same theme can be used. This adds to the potential interest of stamp collecting.

The fact that most of our country's stamps of the past twenty years cannot be sold for face value when offered in quantity is a reflection on the policy of our post office in issuing such large quantities of special issues that philately cannot absorb them.

Let us hope and work for a new policy that will put our stamps in the premium class as are most European issues of recent days.

* * *

Many collectors who plan to become stamp dealers accumulate philatelic material over the years hoping that when the time comes they will have sufficient stock for their purpose. This appears to be a sensible way to prepare for entering the stamp business, but, as in every other venture, there are some rules to follow if success is to be attained.

The market for cheaper stamps of packet grade quality is not now strong, nor is it likely to be so in the future. Soaking ordinary mixtures to acquire quantities of stamps cataloging up to 25¢ each will provide only what every collector is likely to have in surplus. Then, too, the great trend to collecting unused stamps may snowball and virtually eliminate a market for low priced used.

Certain countries will always be more popular than others. Such sidelines as First Day Covers, used Blocks, Margin Imprints, Cancellations, etc., are subject to ups and downs of demand. What is wanted today may be dead tomorrow.

I want to encourage all would-be dealers, but I caution them to have a sound and conservative plan of stock accumulation; for otherwise, when the opportunity comes, they may find themselves with an investment in little-wanted merchandise.

* * *

A man who fastidiously collects coins and as a side hobby formed a collection of Swiss stamps seemed surprised that we could not pay him top price for the souvenir sheets that he had stuck down by their own gum. He protested that we could peel them off the pages if we would take the time.

Another man disregarded the page layout of his albums and without regard for set or chronological arrangement hinged his many thousands of stamps in his album in a hit or miss fashion.

These are just two of the many off-base collectors that I have met lately. Certainly everyone can collect as he or she desires, but as in every other game, there are essential rules to follow in philately. Care of stamps to protect their freshness, neatness or arrangement, proper climate control, careful handling, etc. are basic to every stamp collection. One cannot disregard any of these essential points without paying a high cost when eventually his stamps are sold.

If you ask yourself whether you would pay as much for second quality as you would pay for the very best, you have the answer and also the best reason for taking the best possible care of your stamps.

* * *

For many years I have been writing of the folly of buying current United States stamps in quantities exceeding the requirements of your collecting and correspondence needs. I have called attention to the huge printings, the low face value of the issues, the small historical or memorial value of many issues, the poor artistic execution and, by no means least important, the lack of popularity of these issues abroad. All these and many more reasons indicate that for at least a generation and perhaps much longer current and recent United States stamps when sold in wholesale quantities will not even bring their post office or face value.

Ask youself how you would dispose of $1,000 or $5,000 or more of three, four, and five cent stamps. Industry in the name of economy and efficiency is forced to use postage machines, and individuals rarely use more than a few dollars worth of stamps a month. The fact is that most of us cannot dispose of large quantities of postage even at a discount.

Why do thousands continue to put their excess funds into current United States stamps in the hope of making a profit, a profit as unlikely as anything can be?

If our Government wants to go contrary to good philatelic principles and print all special issues in quantities far exceeding what would make for a good philatelic market, let it do so, but don't you tie up funds in this financial lead weight. Spend your money for older and more seasoned philatelic material where you will have a fair chance of making a gain along with having the joy of owning a worthwhile collection.

* * *

I am indebted to an article in the Saturday Review for knowledge of one of the most important developments of the twentieth century. It is certainly one that is far removed from stamp collecting, but one that might over the next century affect philately along with all the other activities of man. I refer to the work being done by the Rice Research Institute at its Los Banos headquarters in the Philippines.

Ways are here being discovered to more than double the yield of rice per acre. Improved strains of this grain are being developed that will produce higher protein levels in the hope that the exploding populations of Asia might be fed better than were their fathers.

With better farm yields people will be released from the need of producing food. Many will become industrial and service workers. Living standards will improve. Thus the areas of greatest population density on this earth may one day reach the economic level where people have some surplus necessary for luxury. Some will collect stamps, and the market for good philatelic material, always responsive to the addition of collectors, will expand. Certainly, this is long-term thinking, but what is fifty or one hundred years in the history of mankind?

* * *

We are all too pat to classify fellow collectors into rigid categories and then picture them according to our own conception of the category. For instance, if we say, "He is a collector of German stamps," the person who uses Scott's Specialty series is likely to decide that the German collector must be filling spaces in the same type of album. Topical collectors are automatically classified as being uninterested in philately but closely associated with art collectors. This packaging of collectors is 100% wrong. There are no exactly alike collections or collectors.

I have just returned from a trip during which I closely inspected the holdings of 121 collectors and accumulators. Each collection was distinctive in its contents, form of housing, purpose, quality and scope. Of course several used the same albums, but never in quite the same way. Even those patterned collectors, U.S. Plate Block enthusiasts, managed to achieve considerable variety in their presentations.

You cannot picture the typical collection any more than the typical collector can be imagined. This diversity in our fellow philatelists constitutes one of our hobby's greatest virtues. And it insures, too, that no matter how "far out" a collection might be, somewhere there is a market for it.

* * *

Some people are not interested in learning. They have a way of life and don't care to add to it in any way. If they happen to be stamp collectors, the part of the hobby that they are enjoying is sufficient and all the articles published plus all the information available from club or society memberships will not change their form of collecting and certainly it is not my purpose to force change on these people. Let them enjoy stamp collecting in their own way.

There is another and far larger group who takes pride in growth. They strive to expand their knowledge, not only in their selected hobby of philately but in every aspect of life that touches them. The pride of learning means much to these people, and when they can transfer to stamp collecting some of the knowledge that is available to all who will take it, the joy of the hobby is increased greatly.

Fine stamp collections of course require fine stamps, but in addition they reflect the knowledge and ability of their maker. Combining love of philately with philatelic learning results in a far greater return from our hobby than can be gotten by just gathering stamps.

* * *

Most of my readers would be amazed at the number of ex-stamp collectors that there are. These are people who at one time fully enjoyed the hobby, including many who expended large sums on it. They may have dropped out for any number of reasons such as the pressure of business, bad health, financial reverses, displeasure with the action of a dealer, collector or club, etc. Whatever the reason or reasons, we miss them. We particularly miss them if they had either achieved or have the potential for philatelic merit.

These thousands of people are losing an important pleasure by not remaining active stamp collectors. We are losing a broader market for stamps and a greater likelihood of successful stamp organizations by not having them in the fold.

The names of these people are in old membership lists and dealers' files. A real campaign should be mounted to revive their interest. It may be that all some need is a display of interest to get them back. Others may require some sound statistics on the present health of philately. A third group might enjoy meeting with old friends at the club.

This is something for every philatelic organization and business. Let's go to it.

* * *

This is a word to those who worry every time a prominent philatelist dies. They raise the questions, "Who will take his place? Where among the younger generation will we find those sufficiently studious, financially able and with the tremendous love of philately to become great stamp collectors?"

They need not worry. The same questions were asked in 1915 when I was a small boy. They probably were asked in 1895 when my father was a lad. Every generation has its percentage who stand out, who are leaders, who possess the tremendous powers of reasoning and research ability and the drive to see problems through to their solutions.

Today's young stamp collectors are no different from those of years ago. Some are superficial in their attitude towards the hobby, and some are profound. The important thing for this generation is to leave for the next a good clean hobby, uncluttered by petty rackets, unfair practices and excessive speculation.

If we today keep philately sound, the collectors of 1985, 1990 and 2000 will have more than their share of truly great philatelists.

* * *

Fire sirens are to attract attention. When they blast off, we stop, look and listen.

I wish we had a fire siren for stamp collecting because one is badly needed. Certain stamps of so-called hot countries have climbed to the sky due to speculation. They are advertised at prices completely out of line with their true philatelic value. This attracts attention from new collectors who lack the perspective of years of buying stamps and who believe that there is only one way for prices to go; that is up.

Philatelic history is a long pattern of popularity, price rise and bust. There is no reason to believe that the present inflation is any different. Recent stamps that exist in wholesale stocks cannot be rare. If a collector can get particular items in unlimited quantities, they most certainly should not be at ever-rising prices.

The true rarity is difficult to obtain. One must seek it, and then when it is offered, not hesitate about its purchase.

Stamps that are offered in every issue of every magazine are not rarities. They may be and likely are desirable and interesting, and they may fill a space in your album. But after you get your examples, don't fall for the nonsense that increasing prices indicate rarity. Frequently it is the manipulation of insiders that causes this delusion. More often it is the rush of the suckers about to be taken.

* * *

Do we learn from experience? I believe so. The recent Washington International SIPEX Exhibition certainly learned from FIPEX, for it was conducted on a high cultural level in contrast to the 1957 New York Show. The mobs of racing kids and the bourse tables that by their merchandising methods lowered the dignity of stamp collecting were fortunately missing at SIPEX. I am in favor of stamp collecting for all ages, but cannot understand how children in the beginning stage of the hobby can be expected to respect, understand and take part in advanced philately. Do we expect kindergarteners to understand the work of college seniors? Of course not, and there is as much difference between the collecting of the exhibitors at SIPEX and the album of a ten-year-old as there is between first grade arithmetic and quantum theory.

International Exhibitors are for adults, learned in detail, with a depth of knowledge of stamps that the great mass of collectors neither imagine nor care about. Why try to popularize them to those whose sole interest in attending is to acquire a current issue or a First Day Cover?

* * *

It would surprise you to know how many times I have been ushered into the home of a person interested in selling a stamp collection, shown a pile of albums and asked, "How much will you give me for them?" This to my mind is the very poorest way to sell any collection except one that consists of only the very commonest stamps.

All collectors and dealers will agree that condition is the most important factor in determining the worth of stamps. To be sure of their condition, important items must be examined in a laboratory with black light, enlargers, and other scientific equipment. To assume offhand that there are no repairs or flaws in a valuable stamp is to invite possible future regrets.

We all know that many imitations and counterfeits exist. No stamp authority can carry in his head all the points that must be checked to determine the status of a large variety of material.

Some collections are figured by catalog value, some by face value and some by the buyer's reference to his records of prices realized on past sales. A hasty cataloging or counting can never be accurate. To be done correctly, such work requires both time and patience. Certainly the price records of the purchasing dealer are apt to be voluminous and not readily transportable to wherever the collection may be.

In our opinion the only kind of valuation that is apt to be given under hurry-up circumstances in surroundings removed from a reference library is one that is on the low side. After all, one cannot expect the buyer to overpay on a gamble.

We recommend to those who have stamps to sell that they choose a responsible buyer and then permit the buyer to take a reasonable length of time to examine the material involved, preferably at the buyers headquarters where by the use of his laboratory, library and office equipment a conclusion of price can be reached that is not the "Stealing Price" of many hasty deals.

* * *

The reason why a fine stamp collection with substantial value embracing almost any philatelic category will realize more when sold by a good auction house is explainable in a simple arithmetic lesson.

The important and valuable parts of a collection, that is, those singles, sets, covers and blocks, etc., that have individual scarcity and more demand than supply, seldom constitute as much as fifty percent of the total catalog value involved. In other words, almost every collection includes a high percentage of low-and medium-priced items that are readily obtainable from many dealers.

The choice pieces in the collection can be sold by any method for a good price. They, in a well run auction, reach the cream of buyers and thus they bring a level of realization that will please almost any vendor. But, then what of the balance of the collection which in point of proportion of catalog is very important?

In auction selling, a huge market for country collections, remainder lots, and odds and ends exists so that the unimportant and somewhat overlooked balance does its share to bring the total net realization to as much as fifty percent more than can be obtained by an outright sale.

It is true that it takes three or four months to sell through auctions, but isn't it worth waiting for so much more handsome a return?

* * *

I marvel at the "hot country collectors." They are a special breed. They find time to memorize the latest bid and ask prices for Carmania or whatever other country is currently being run up by the insiders. They know exactly how much their holdings advanced in value during the last forty-eight hours and sometimes they have even plotted on graph paper the future of their paper earnings. They are truly a wonderful lot, but as most stock gamblers they usually neglect to count the duds they acquire during the pursuit of what's sizzling at the minute.

Speculators and plungers do a service for stamp collecting. They provide the source of supply for later years and this is quite important. The stamp trade cannot afford to carry the huge investment that would be required to assure the new collector of 1986 or 1996 that he can fill his wants.

But when one of the speculatively inclined stamp collectors tells me, as they frequently do, that he cannot spare the time to study the older and classic stamps, or that forming a first-rate collection is for patsies, not a shrewd investor such as he is, I begin to wonder. I wonder what we have done wrong in the selling of philately, its pleasures and recompensations that so many of its followers can only read a dollar sign where it says "Stamp Collecting, the World's Greatest Hobby."

* * *

There is no one best way to collect stamps. Neither is there one best reason for collecting. Watching a ten-year-old boy or girl dream of things beyond his or her reach as each turns the pages of an album is one way to understand the grasp that stamp collecting has for those who will participate. At the other end is the elderly person who has enjoyed the lore of philately during a long life that has been busy and fruitful.

In between are millions who seek in stamps the myriad benefits that they offer including learning, companionship, economic return, mental health.

It is true that the great majority of stamp collections when measured against the giants of the hobby are inconsequential; but it is just as true that in the hours that were spent on their albums the return to every collector was enormous without regard to the size or scope of his efforts.

A hobby fully enjoyed is of benefit beyond measure. Stamp collecting can be and is enjoyed by millions of followers to the great advantage of every one of them.

* * *

Pity poor John Doe. He has been saving stamps for over forty years, always with the thought that in addition to the pleasures he received his collection would have sufficient value that when sold at the end of his life it would result in a large estate. In his other activities John Doe showed great shrewdness. He joined trade associations and civic clubs so that he could keep abreast of the times and know the best procedures for personal gains. But in stamp collecting he just saved stamps. He didn't attend stamp exhibitions to see how the other fellow was doing it. He didn't subscribe to a good philatelic journal to read about trends in collecting. He didn't even read the introduction to the annual catalogs where much useful advice was available.

He carefully calculated the annual increases in catalog value of his collection and based his success as a stamp collector on the growth of that total. Unheeded were the little boxes that Scott inserts in the catalog referring to condition being an important factor in value.

And so the years went by and John Doe, through some purchases, much envelope peeling and an occasional gift from a friend, accumulated a closetful of albums and boxes with a catalog value in a very high number of dollars. When his doctor suggested that Doe's days were numbered he decided to cash in on his stamps.

Yes, you can pity him for the shock of learning that today's collectors desire fine quality and that stamp dealers already have far too much common material in stock. But then anyone who blindly follows a course in any activity invites a blow of this sort.

* * *

We advocate collecting stamps in sound condition with attractive appearance. But one thing we cannot understand is why those who cannot afford the cost of premium stamps are expected to forego placing in their albums the best they can afford.

Most people collect for pleasure. If they enjoy completing, say, the U.S. 1869 issue and cannot afford $2,500 for a super-duper ninety cents, why should they keep the space empty when a lesser specimen can be obtained for $250. It is true that if they later offer their $250 stamp for resale it will not bring a premium price, but it will sell in accordance with its quality and no doubt produce a fair return. Best of all the collector had the pleasure of owning a desirable stamp.

The fetish of condition is fine for the few who can buy it. If it deprives many others of some of stamp collecting's great enjoyment, it is harmful when overdone. To expect early United States stamps in only perfectly centered full gum condition to be available in quantity for every prospective collector is to blindly ignore the facts of how they were produced, issued and preserved through the years.

The very few that are available are priced too low at today's prices. The majority of collectors should forget about them and concentrate on obtaining stamps in the average condition in which they were issued. These they can afford and can obtain.

* * *

The worth of stamp collecting to society is primarily in the incentive it creates to learning. It has the flavor of school, lectures, reading, writing, art, and economics without being any of these things. The ten-year-old with his five dollar album cannot escape the above any more than the middle-aged, well-to-do collector who uses stamps to fill his surplus time and take some of his excess wealth into a more interesting direction than the stock market.

Every stamp in a collection offers a path to increased knowledge. There is no better clean, wholesome and accepted avocation. Why is it then that we hear talk that stamp collecting isn't recruiting followers as in the past. Can it be that the dollar sign in all the sensational press releases and articles in the lay press discourages new prospects? Of course, we delight in the knowledge that some "Daddy Warbucks" paid many thousand dollars for some rarity. But to 99%-plus of collectors it means nothing more than the ability to say that they also collect stamps. Frankly the thousand-dollar items are wonderful to deal in or own but common sense indicates that the handful of potential buyers for them could never affect the hobby except in its rarified upper strata where few of us belong financially. It is a fact that stamp collecting can be fully enjoyed for just about as little cost as any other hobby known. When will some journal of wide distribution get the message and print an authentic article based on the real worth and value of stamp collecting to over 99% of its followers.?

* * *

In a few cities in the United States stamp collectors have established permanent and attractive meeting places. The New York Collectors Club has its fine building on East 35th St. The clubs of Portland, Oregon, Seattle, Washington and Los Angeles have either buildings or offices that are exclusively for the use of the club members. There are others around the country. There are many advantages to this arrangement including being able to maintain a useful library, having a place to meet fellow collectors at any hour, adding to the local prestige of philately, etc.

Early in this century the Philadelphia Stamp Club maintained permanent rooms in the center of the city for many years. The membership of this club included important and busy people who perhaps could seldom visit the club but realized the advantages of membership and considered their dues a small contribution to the cause. During the Depression the club slipped into the inactive status and the meeting rooms were given up.

Today stamp collecting is stronger than ever with many active people enjoying its benefits. The large cities of America are in need of full-time stamp collectors' clubs with attractive quarters.

Busy philatelists who may enjoy attendance at these club rooms only a few times a year could benefit from them the same as the retired oldster who might drop by every day. The costs would not be beyond the value of the advantages.

I hope to see soon such local philatelic headquarters in all large cities. They are well worth the effort needed to establish them.

* * *

On July 22nd we are having an unusual gathering at our offices. It will be of about twenty boys ages eleven to fifteen from the poorest section of the city. I doubt if any of these lads ever even heard of stamp collecting, but we plan to present to them a program that will arouse excitement and curiosity that may make a few collectors.

We will show them the stamps of a variety of countries and how one can see the other fellow's way of life through stamps. We will explain the relationship between collecting stamps and the normal acquisitive inclinations of most people.

The program is planned to last about two hours and will be presented by a member of our staff who, when he joined us five years ago, knew as little about the hobby as the boys he will be talking to do now.

We do not believe in giving stamps to children to make them into collectors. It is our belief that the children must put something of themselves into acquiring what is needed to follow philately. Accordingly, we hope to establish some kind of an exchange of services with these boys that will earn for them the stamps and albums needed by them.

If only five of these deprived youngsters are made wider-eyed by philately our efforts will be well justified. Making them aware and desirous to know is a small contribution for us to make to society.

* * *

Almost every community in the United States has its United Fund. Through this agency money is raised to support the many needed social services our government permits to remain in private management. If each of these agencies had its own drive for money, the cost of raising the money would be several times that of a combined drive. In addition, there would be the annoyances of being approached frequently and writing many checks for contributions. Almost everyone agrees that the United Fund drive is a good arrangement.

How is it that we haven't adopted its lessons to collecting? There are philatelists who pay dues to as many as 20 or 30 different organizations in our hobby not because they follow the specialties of most of them but because they assume the responsibility of supporting all of the hobby's branches. Even lesser collectors usually carry a half dozen membership cards. Most of the organizations represented by these memberships are weak. They depend on volunteer workers to keep them going. Much of the dues received is dissipated in duplication of the work of every other group.

How about the idea of a United Philately of America? Within it every group could function for its special purpose, but the centralized organization would assume the financial and administrative details together with editorial and publication tasks that now are scattered. Isn't this worth thinking about?

* * *

I have known him for over twenty-five years. During all that time and probably for some years previous he was a liberal and regular purchaser of philatelic items. While a good part of his interest was in covers bearing postmarks of his own dearly beloved state, he maintained a warm feeling for many other stamp collecting areas and it was as likely as not that his auction bid sheets would list offers for items from many different countries. So he acquired and piled high a truly large collection.

Now at the age when vigor and eyesight were weakened he admitted that some of his albums hadn't been opened in more than ten years. The contents of drawers of duplications and unmounted material that overflowed their capacities filled a good part of his attic. He agreed that even if he had the vitality he couldn't inventory all his material within the next year or two. He most certainly lacked the vitality.

I advised that he commence selling portions of his collections, particularly those that he hadn't looked at in years. This would serve several purposes: One, to reduce the problem that his family, who were unacquainted with stamps, would face in obtaining the best possible realization for his estate. Two, to put back on the market items much sought after and seldom available, so that newer collectors could enjoy their possession. Three, to provide a cash fund that would be available to pay the tax on the part of the collection he retained, for inheritance taxes are as inevitable as death.

For, hard as it is to realize, you must plan for your eventual demise.

* * *

I doubt that the old-time saying, "At some time or other every boy collects stamps," is true today. Many children do collect stamps but not every one or probably even fifty percent of them. I don't believe all children are born collectors, inclined towards saving things of interest to them.

I do believe that when the world of the collector is opened up to them they get a wider vision of life. Touching a stamp from China, looking at a coin from ancient Greece or moving a chess piece of African ivory can have a vast influence on the average curious child, if accompanying the action is an explanation of its significance. Our stamp albums for children fall down in not placing the space for specific stamps around the exciting story that each stamp can have.

It isn't necessary to print an album for 50,000 varieties nor, for new collectors, to house every stamp issued by a country. It isn't even desirable to do so. A fresh look at album publishing might call for the issuance of a magazine-type of album on a monthly basis and formed around stories of stamps geared to the particular age group concerned.

The adult collectors of the next generation will come mostly from the child collectors of today. Can we afford to overlook any constructive means of interesting them in the life-long enjoyment of stamp collecting?

* * *

Everywhere I go I hear from stamp club members that they are unsuccessful in their efforts to get the support of many of the outstanding collectors of their city. Frequently the leading collectors are the busiest people in town and are already obligated to civic organizations that must take priority over pleasurable ones. Sometimes, too, they don't care for philatelic publicity because they fear that this might attract burglars. There are also, of course, people who are antisocial, and if they wish to enjoy solitary philately that is certainly their privilege. However, a little soul-searching by the leaders of the club will usually result in the conclusion that they aren't offering any good reasons for these people to join with them.

Meetings that are dull and dominated by petty business, by discussions of the latest United States commemorative or some minor perforation fault aren't going to convince a busy executive that he should become a club member. He expects and requires more than a repetition of what he can learn from Scott's Catalog if you are to interest him.

Stir up your meetings. Don't be afraid of controversial discussion. Don't hesitate to put all the business in the hands of an executive committee. Scout around and develop new ideas for excellent programs. When it becomes known that the stamp club is lively, you will be amazed at how attractive it will become to those who now ignore it.

* * *

It isn't often that I condemn a competitor's business methods, but when I do it is almost always because stamp speculation is being accentuated by the one involved. Lately I have met several collectors who suppose themselves to be "investing" by the systematic arrangement of sending a fixed sum monthly to a dealer. This fellow claims to be clairvoyant about future values and thus able to select for them stamps that will increase in value within a short time. (Of course, the greatest stamp experts of all times never had such an ability.) The "investors" in these schemes are usually poor people, limited in their finances and all too eager to strike it rich with a few dollars skimped from the family budget.

The small print of the promoter's proposition is overlooked or, if read, is not completely understandable to anyone but a lawyer. The victims are totally unaware of real values, of the fact that most stamps must advance at least 100% in net market price for the collector to be able to recover his cost in selling to the trade, and that the few items he will acquire from the promoter that do advance will be heavily outweighed by the many that don't increase in value.

Promoters such as these lack the philatelic ability to sell stamps for the pleasure and learning they give the collector. They in fact have no personal appreciation of the joys of philately or they wouldn't attempt to undermine the hobby with harmful schemes.

* * *

It is becoming increasingly difficult to get very much for a dollar. The "good old days" of the 5 & 10¢ store that later became the 25 & 50¢ store and now are again the 5 & 10 (but dollars instead of cents) are gone forever. I can think of nothing but stamp collecting that can be indulged in today for pennies. The old "nickel rocket" baseball is now $2.00. The golf club that charged $75 a year is now $375. Movies in center city are $4.50 and up.

Only in stamp collecting are some things available for pennies. Yes, thousands of stamps can be bought for less than a dime each, and, best of all, included in this bonanza are some of the world's most interesting varieties. While it is doubtful if these lower-priced stamps can be obtained individually at such low prices, in collections and groups practically all are available.

This means that stamp collecting can be introduced to newcomers at a lower cost than any similar hobby. It doesn't imply that valuable collections can be formed for a few cents, but certainly they can be interesting and informative. With ingenuity and enterprise they can be developed into potentially exhibitable properties, not to compete in rarity but to attract the attention of others to a project worth understanding and developing. Most stamp firms could not exist solely on the income from small sales. They must develop a rarity trade and business volume to provide the profit margin required. However, small buyers who understand the economics of these times can, by judiciously accumulating their funds until a sizeable purchase can be made, find many stamp dealers anxious for their trade.

* * *

For the past week I have been listening to people comment on the presidential election, the candidates, and the issues. It is simply pitiful to contemplate the amount of misconception, misunderstanding and willful misrepresentation concerning the statements of all the candidates.

We have a similar condition in the stamp trade. Every catalog or advertisement states what is meant by its descriptive terms. An item or lot described as v.g. (meaning very good) is not far up on the condition pole, as v.g. is in most catalogs definitely stated to be a lot with minor faults. Now it makes no difference what you, the individual, mean by v.g. You must, in fairness, accept the terms of the seller as stated in his catalog. He is not about to ship fine merchandise for a v.g. description just because you think that term should mean fine. On the other hand, nearly everyone in the stamp business will cheerfully make refund for true errors that they have made in description. Please, for the sake of your own satisfaction, read carefully all the small print explanations of what you may expect if you send orders or bids to any stamp dealer. Don't try to make their terminology fit your interpretation. All conditions must be construed as the seller explains his grading.

There will be a great increase in the harmony in our country if people will be more careful in making judgment of statements of public figures. So, too, will your satisfaction in stamps be greater if you refrain from bidding on good quality when you intend to buy only fine or very fine.

* * *

It is time to stop downgrading stamp collecting. Certainly, a seven-year-old can be a collector of stamps without really having the least idea of its purpose; but, in the main, when we refer to stamp collectors, we refer to those who understand to some extent the complicated pattern into which our avocation has advanced.

We are no longer queer individuals peeling foreign-stamps from wastebasket findings and glueing them into albums. In fact, we haven't been doing that for close to a century. We are, if we fit the design of most philatelists and embryo philatelists, people who, through the study and classification of the rules, regulations, publications and emissions of the postal services of the world are adding to historic knowledge and understanding. We can and do arrive at concepts of worldly development and progress; economic, educational and otherwise, as a result of research, into postal communications systems.

Gone forever are the days when we measure a stamp collection by its size. Gone should be the desire on the part of some of us to possess certain stamps just so we can gain applause for our display of wealth. Today is the day of utilizing philately as a method and, in fact, as a motive, to increase awareness, greater learning, and a fuller understanding of the many nations and races of this fascinating world.

* * *

Where in the world do you find champions of anything who don't seriously practice their field through long days, weeks and years? A man doesn't become champion tennis player of the world or a great golfer, nor does he write excellent novels or fine poetry, without long effort. The few with the stamina and natural ability to excel must add to nature's gifts the will and necessary work. It is quite common to find people in occupations removed from philately who devote seventy and eighty hours a week to their subject.

Now, turning to stamp collecting; at almost every show there are disappointed exhibitors who regret not earning the awards they wanted. They sometimes justify their expectations by pointing to rarities in their frames. But the real point at issue is, can they demonstrate that they should have won by reason of studying and learning all there is to know about the subject they choose to exhibit? Have they added anything to published knowledge? Are they prepared by way of having observed and checked quantities of material to defend the position they take as to the meaning of their write-ups?

These and other factors must be considered and pursued if you intend to be a prize-winning philatelist. If you are unwilling or unable to follow the path of champions, be content with lesser rewards.

* * *

For perhaps as long as seventy-five years one form of stamp selling has been to offer "Collections by Country" advertised as collector-made. These are usually arranged by dealers who break albums along country or sectional lines and, after judicious removal of the prime material (complete better sets, special cancellations, nice covers, etc.), put a price on the remainder. Since figured in the catalog value are the plentiful varieties that couldn't be sold individually, the overall price received by the dealer is better than straight mathematics would indicate. From the viewpoint of the collector buyer, however, even if he must pay for a percentage of duplication or common items, "Country Collections" offer an excellent way to make a good showing fast at a reduced cost from that of buying each stamp individually.

Collectors should exercise care to buy collections that are not packed with high catalog value seconds, revenue cancellations or repaired items. Since it is a relatively easy matter to take a ready-made packet of, say, 1,000 different Austria, transfer it to pages and add a dozen or so high catalog value, poor quality items acquired in a damaged lot, the temptation to do so exists with a few dealers. The profit of taking the packet that catalogs about $100 and costs about $14 plus the dozen "dogs" cataloging $200 and costing $10 and then selling the package for 20% of Scott or $60 is readily apparent.

Legitimate collector-made collections are priced by knowing dealers in accordance with the factors of completeness, condition, scarcity and demand. When so priced, they offer a reasonable and sound basis for building an interesting, informative, and pleasing collection.

* * *

Once upon a time there was a collector who saved all kinds of stamps—postage, revenue, seals, labels—everything. Then he was influenced to cut down, so he collected only postage stamps, until he further retrenched and saved stamps of just one continent. This being quite a broad field, he after a while narrowed it to one country. By and by, he became infatuated by one issue of the country and for a time studied only that series until, lo and behold, he discovered that one of the denominations was most unusual. That being the case, he devoted all his philatelic time to that denomination alone. One day he came across a printing variety of the favored stamp that he identified as having been printed from a certain position on the plate. This being information that had been hitherto unchronicled, he again pondered upon his philatelic future and decided to specialize in this one position of his favorite stamp from the most interesting set put out by a certain country in a continent he knew to be a part of a vast world—and then, because he couldn't find anything to add to his collection, he quit collecting.

* * *

SOJEX, NOJEX, SEPAD, BALPEX, COMPEX, NOPEX, FLAMEX, BNAPEX, SUNPEX, STAMPEX, SEAPEX, BANGPEX, REPEX, etc., etc. The coined names of stamp exhibitions seem like words from a new language, one that ends all its nouns with "EX." The only one of these names that is readily understandable is STAMPEX, used by the Salem, Oregon club and for an annual exhibition in London, England.

I wonder how much good these acronyms do for publicity. Just how many non-collectors recognize their meaning? Probably very few. While the intention is to create a short, snappy title, its lack of meaning to most of the public defeats the aim of intriguing outsiders to come to the "...EX."

It is my belief that the simple title, "Philadelphia Stamp Show" or "Exhibition of New Jersey Stamp Collectors," while much longer, is well worth the additional space it takes up.

* * *

It is interesting to listen to two or more advanced specialists discuss their favorite philatelic subject. The best part of listening is in hearing them express opinions that frequently are not in agreement. If they are the calm type, they do so in a friendly manner, but if they are dogmatic people you may watch the sparks fly.

We know that there is disagreement to be found among people on any subject, and stamp collecting is no exception. The lack of uniform opinion often extends even to the great experts, and many philatelic questions remain unresolved even after years of study because the experts differ.

I have seen items labeled false by those who believed they knew all the answers. Later, the same items turned out to be genuine in the judgment of a new generation of scholars. Of course, the reverse is also true. While we do possess much positive knowledge there are some things we don't know, or at best are only speculating about, when we hazard an answer. In the light of this, let us all be tolerant and open-minded about the details of our hobby that are somewhat murky. The best that we can do in those cases is guess at what is right.

* * *

At lunch today a man asked me what a collection is worth. That's almost like asking, "How long is a piece of string?" To get an answer that has meaning you must refer to a specific collection or piece of string.

There are two values to any collection: what it is worth to the owner and what it will bring when sold in the marketplace. An owner's value includes such things as cost, sentimental attachment, continued interest in the collection and other matters important only to the particular owner.

The market value cannot reflect any of these things. It has to be based on an unemotional, realistic decision: "What will a collector pay for it?" Merchants, to exist, need a profit over and above cost of goods and overhead. While some operate on a closer margin than others, philately is a business with a high labor factor. It is rare that the total markup needed is less than a department store requires. Therefore you must assume that, for your collection, the value it has to you as an active collector will not be the value to others when it is offered for sale.

* * *

Somewhere there may be a collection of only the very finest quality material, but I have never seen such. Every collector should acquire the best stamps he can afford. Even in the albums of the most fastidious and affluent, though, you will find a few items that are not top quality. Frequently the problem is simple unavailability. Scarce stamps by definition exist in limited numbers. Production methods were often so crude that few first-rate stamps were ever available. Age and handling have served to damage many that started out as sound.

The greatest problem arises with those who think that they have only perfect copies. Often they are the victims of the unscrupulous or ignorant.

There have been for years in most countries expert repairers who doctor or alter "cripples," making them appear to be what they are not. Some of the work done by these "artists" is so slick that it fools all but the most expert philatelists.

Wise stamp buyers patronize dealers whom they know to have the knowledge and equipment that exposes "restorations." Ethical dealers sell such items for precisely what they are and at the much reduced price they are worth.

* * *

I was much dismayed several years ago when I learned that an uncle had burned all the correspondence in an estate he was managing. Some of it dated back to the Civil War. I believed that my uncle, who was well aware that I was a stamp dealer, should have known better. And yet what had I ever done to avail him of philatelic information? Of course, in a vague way, I may have at times mentioned that collectors of stamps also value postmarks and envelopes that have gone through the mails. But I never showed him any examples of what we save or told him why. This is an all too common story. Many of those outside our hobby think of us as eccentrics who play with bits of paper. Rarely do they associate us with students of history, economics, travel, art, etc. And it's our fault, because we have done very little to enlighten them. Uncles will continue to burn up old papers as long as we hide from them the true story of philately, its ramifications and great diversity of interest.

* * *

One of the things that all of us do is eat. Food is both a necessity and a pleasure. Its production is our greatest industry, including activities from the farm to the table. Each nation develops its favorite forms of food and they become so-called "national dishes." Considering some of the relatively unimportant things that our Post Office has commemorated in special issues, the food industry has been neglected. Of course there have been a "chicken" stamp and a 4-H stamp, etc., but there hasn't been a stamp for the great American steak or corn on the cob. We consume millions of hot dogs. Why not a stamp for this delicious tidbit? Our cold winter days are made more bearable by such things as Philadelphia Pepper Pot Soup, hot baked potatoes, rolls fresh from the oven or Boston Baked Beans. New Orleans has had a reputation for fine food for over a century. I believe a series of stamps celebrating the great American dishes of all parts of the country would be desirable. What do you say, Mr. Postmaster General?

* * *

Those stamp collectors who get all their information from newspaper stamp columns often believe that the entire hobby rests on obtaining new issues as they appear. The newspaper columns cannot be faulted in this because new issues are news and that is what the paper is all about.

It so happens that stamp collection is a hobby with hundreds of angles. The ways to collect are almost as varied as the number of collectors. Some collectors do as they do because they lack a broad vision of the hobby. These are usually the people who are exposed to only a limited range of philatelic reading. They never acquaint themselves with that which doesn't already cross their notice.

Subscription to at least one and preferably several stamp journals is a necessity if you want to get a broad picture of the hobby. Considering the low cost of such publications, even the poorest stamp collector can afford this educational influence. And yet among your stamp collecting acquaintances there will be some who never read anything but the local paper's report of new issues.

* * *

We are indeed fortunate that postage stamps were not invented until 1840. Just suppose the ancient peoples had used adhesives to pay for the carriage of mail. Since the Western World was then divided into duchies, baronies, dukedoms and principalities in almost limitless number, the variety of stamps would be beyond comprehension. Let us imagine stamps in the city states of Greece. They alone were more in number than the countries in present-day Europe. If Sparta issued a commemorative set for its army, Athens would have believed itself obligated to issue an equally long and attractive set memorializing Plato or Diogenes. Or again, as Hannibal progressed through Spain, the Pyrenees, Gaul and over the Alps, Carthage could have flooded the world with a set showing each elephant on a separate value. The income from such an issue might have been enough to save Carthage from its later collapse. I am sure you get some idea of what stamp collecting would now be had Rowland Hill been a Carthaginian.

* * *

If I wasn't so busy as a stamp dealer there would be many specialties in our hobby that I would like to have collected. But rent and salaries, insurance and telephone bills generally forbade retaining for my pleasure what could be sold to meet expenses.

I have always had a love for stamps issued previous to my birth in 1905. They seem to represent a time beyond my reach, just as distant countries to which one might never journey have a fascination for many collectors. The splendid engraving of many Victorian British Colonies, the crude printing of some early South American stamps, the wonderful Germany and Italian States issues and our own first issue revenues are never tiring to me. I can find endless variety in the later 19th century issues of quite a few countries, notably China, Turkey, Norway and New Zealand.

To me, these and other stamps issued before my time are fascinating for their history, typography and the difficulty of securing fine specimens. I'll forego the latest pictorials any day for a chance to work with pre-1905 stamps.

* * *

In 1930, when we commenced this business, there were many cover collectors. They collected covers that were from unusual places, bore scarce postmarks, had interesting illustrations, or exhibited some historical significance such as rates, postal routes or franking. In almost all cases the collectors of that time sought early covers and had little interest in the then current post office products.

We still have many such collectors, but for each one of them there is a regiment of collectors of current postal history, that is First Day and cacheted event covers covering all the phases of present-day life. In 1920, when the late Philip Ward, Jr. tried to sell Pilgrim Tercentenary First Day Covers at the Philadelphia Stamp Club, most of the members gave him the "Bronx Cheer." As one of those who turned him down at the time I must admit my lack of vision.

In like fashion there are continual innovations in our hobby. It is obvious that few of us can get in on all the new fads, but experience tells us that some of them will have strong and healthy followings long beyond our days.

* * *

The library in my apartment is limited by the space available. When I had a house I had a few thousand volumes. Now there are but a thousand. You might ask how I decided what to retain and on what basis do I add to it?

There are many books of current interest that I read and pass along to others for their enjoyment. They have no permanent reference value, so I must forbid them a fixed place in my library. When I reduced the size of the library the sole determining factor was anticipated need of the book to look up a fact or to refresh my knowledge of a subject. I parted with many books that had been old friends, companions to both my father and myself. The affection that I had for them was deep-felt, but it had to be terminated. Their space was needed by more practical and useful volumes.

Perhaps your stamp collection is similar to this. Many of your old friends, items that you cherish, are no longer relevant to your present philatelic status. It might be heartrending to sort out this material for disposal, but, as with my books, it is cheering to think the new owners are receiving full measure of the pleasures they can give.

* * *

I am continually saddened by elderly retired people who possess fine active minds, yet do nothing but await the closing of their days. They retired without a plan for keeping busy. They have plenty of time and it has become their worst enemy. I recently talked to a man in this situation. He almost cried because of the emptiness of his days. I asked him if he had ever tried to list the things he was capable of doing within the confines of his town. Following his answer that no one wants an old man I ran down a list of old men's jobs that are everywhere. They include motel sitter, ticket collector at events, shopper for shut-ins, adviser to small businesses in the line he had followed all his life and others. I assured him there was more than one useful job he could do. I could have suggested that he take up a hobby—stamp collecting, gardening, puzzling, etc., but in his case I believe a financial incentive is needed. I hope he listened to me. I hope everyone in the same situation will give it thought and resume a purpose in life.

* * *

No doubt many of us have had the experience of being invited to view a friend's collection and finding that he has a lot of poor quality stamps. His boast that he was 90% complete in U.S. is true if we consider spaces filled, but most of us are beyond seeking only to fill spaces. We want attractive, complete stamps, without missing corners, with reasonable centering and fresh color. What do we say to our friend collector under these circumstances? Do we chance hurting his feelings by pointing out that he should collect better examples or do we pat him on the back and congratulate him on his accumulation of seconds? Well, I suppose it depends on how well you know him and how much courage you have at the particular time. For my part, I try to give a lesson on quality. I select one of the best stamps in the lot and say, "If only all your stamps were that nice you would have something." This will elicit questions and each answer should be directed toward the need to collect only first quality stamps. This is not only because of the value involved. It is because eye appeal and satisfaction can rarely be found in any but nice things. Our first duty is to inform all collectors that quality is the most important element in philatelic value.

* * *

The best in any endeavor rarely comes about by chance. Hard work must usually be combined with talent if the goal is first place. Years of study, practice and stick-to-itiveness are the past history of all top accomplishments. Yet in stamp collecting we find quite a few people who firmly believe that all they need to do is buy a few scarce stamps and mount them on pages in order to form a prize-winning collection.

None of the thousands of fine volumes of philatelic literature embracing studies of practically every stamp are ever cracked by these people. I have even heard them say, "I detest write-up on pages." They miss completely the great and perhaps ultimate goal of philately: learning through stamps. Frequently the only thing they see is a series of dollar signs attached to each of their possessions.

Philately is an art along with being a hobby and diversion. Mastery of the art is required if you will be one of the best and that mastery is obtainable only if you will study and read about your stamps. Then can you hope to arrange them with the expression of knowledge that makes you deserving of a first award.

* * *

There are many really scarce stamps that have a low selling price. The reason is that there is small demand for them. They may come from unpopular countries, be minor varieties from places that lack a specialist's following, or they may be for sale in a part of the world where the collectors don't take to that type of stamps.

Some of the Latin American countries have a fascinating history, both postal and otherwise. Their stamps are attractive and tell interesting stories. Because of poor economic, social and educational levels the home market of collectors is quite limited. Under such circumstances stamps that exist in very small quantities might sell at the same prices as items issued in the millions by a more progressive and richer nation.

However, times change, and the backward country of today may be a world leader in time to come. There are many wise collectors who have recognized this and enjoyed building a collection of an unpopular country, knowing that the spin of the wheel could sooner or later change its status.

* * *

You are sorting stamps and suddenly pick up one with a full town cancellation that is perfectly struck, the one in a thousand. What do you do? I have a friend who mounts such an item with a write-up of the town, its history and particularly what it was like at the time of the use of the stamp. He may take several pages to set down all that he learns because the stamp and its cancel stimulated his curiosity.

Another collector might apply the same kind of study to the subject of a stamp or the frame design. There are those who endlessly investigate types of paper or ink or perforation.

Then how about printing methods, postal rates, mail routes, enabling legislation, quantity ordered, distribution, types of use, supply in collectors' hands and range of price? There is no end to what you can build up around a single stamp—any stamp from any country. Thus there is no reason ever to grow stale on philately.

* * *

I enjoy looking at maps and have ever since, as a small boy, I found in an old book a map of the Boer War campaigns. The names of the places seemed ever so strange to my youthful understanding. I pictured Orange Free State as a place that must have originated my favorite fruit. Such cities as Bloemfontein, Mafeking and Vryburg aroused visions of wild Zulus and Hottentots doing war dances. My ignorance of the world was really stupendous. A few years later, when I discovered stamp collecting and then the use of encyclopedias to find the answers to questions, I was on my way to a life that has never been dull. With stamps, my Britannica, and my map collection I can fill in any free time I ever have in the fully enjoyable game of classifying the stamps, reading about their subjects and finding the exact places where they were used or, if unused, were available for postal service.

Every collector has a great love for some part of his philatelic activity. I hope it brings all of you as much pleasure as mine has to me.

* * *

David Lidman's stamp column in the *New York Times* of July 19th, 1970 carries an article entitled "Fujeira—Where is it?." Geographically, its location can be pinpointed to the Oman Peninsula of Arabia. Postally it is a different matter. The handful of people who live there must be the world's greatest letter writers. How else could they need between 90 and 100 new varieties of stamps between May 12th and June 25th of this year? The post office cost of one of each of these would be $53.21. Quite a nice income if many are sold, particularly for a country of less than 20,000 population, of whom perhaps 2,000 at the most can read or write.

It is probable that almost none of these alleged stamps ever reach Fujeira. They go directly from the printer to wholesale stamp channels. They take money from uninformed collectors that could go for issues of more discretionary countries.

It behooves every one of us to warn all collectors away from this junk, and Fujeira is not the only such junk-issuing country.

Stamp collecting must be based on stamps issued by established governments that realize their responsibilities to maintain postal service and issue such stamps as are required by the service and politics of the place.

* * *

Ours is not a fuddy-duddy diversion. It is loaded with appeal to fully alive active people. It is the only reasonable way for a sportsman to have a collection of handsome sporting pictures. It certainly can offer warriors and military historians more visions of battles, maneuvers and that great result of war—boundary changes—than any other collecting diversion. Are you interested in city planning? Just look carefully at stamps showing street scenes from around the world. Is your concern social service? Stamps dedicated to all phases of social uplift exist by the hundreds. Any good collection of these or other topics can be dramatized, even to planning a stage skit around it. Such a program can be used to entertain Rotary, Kiwanis, Lions and other service clubs. Your church or synagogue will be delighted to hear an interesting and exciting philatelic talk before the men's club or some other unit.

When you put on the talk prepare in advance. Do not rely only on the dollar value of your stamps. Other things than stamps have value, but no other collecting field has our color. Let's accentuate the positive and publicize our great assets.

* * *

This year stamp collecting has received a great deal of valuable publicity from the sale at auction of the famous British Guiana rarity. We all delight in this, but one flash is not enough. We have informed the world that there are rare stamps and that some rich people will pay huge sums to obtain them. A bigger task remains. It is to tell the great middle class American family that there is no better family hobby than stamp collecting. That it is one that appeals to all ages. We must tell them that as little as a dollar or two a week is sufficient to bring them, parents and children alike, a wonderland of joy, learning and togetherness.

Men and women who enjoy stamp collecting are everywhere. So too are children, who get the feel of history and geography in an exciting way from stamps. This being so, a joint collecting effort by the young and old of a household can probably, next to church activities, do the most to keep the family together. If we can in some way get this message across to millions of American families they will thank all of us for many years to come.

* * *

Two men, to their surprise, recently met in our office and greeted one another with, "What are you doing here?" They were old friends, in fact had played bridge and golf together for more than twenty years. Each one was a steady buyer in our auctions for an equally long time. Their wives were kafeeklatsch pals, and their children went to the same schools. Yet neither knew of the other's interest in philately.

There must be much of this lack of knowing who collects. Within a small area of suburban Philadelphia, we send almost a hundred auction catalogs. Several of the recipients have remarked to me, "If only there were some other collectors near where I live." If the facts were known, an amazing number of adult collectors could be found in almost every community.

Don't hesitate to mention stamp collecting in any group of people. You will be certain of starting many warm friendships in that way.

* * *

It is probable that everyone has a secret self that isn't bared even on the psychiatrist's couch. Our thoughts are often such that we would be embarrassed to make them public. On the other hand, many of the ideas, judgements, desires and hopes that cross our minds are useful and constructive, well worth all the publicity we can give them. How is one to decide what is to be shut up in himself and what is to be made public property?

It must be admitted that far too much is made public property that should never get beyond the meditations of its originator. Ideas need a proper time for blooming. They need a careful refinement from the original flash that creates them. They should be checked much as a research scientist looks at every possibility presented by his work. If the right checks are made, the time is ripe and the proper presentation is made, the casual idea can become the thought that moves the universe or at least changes something—preferably in a desirable way.

The above, of course, applies as well to philatelic thoughts. Many should be discarded before they are a minute old and no doubt some are. But if you get a good one—one that is founded on fact and is practicable, out with it. Philately is waiting for the stimulation that can come only from such a source.

* * *

We have all heard the cry "I'm going to retire soon and what will I do to kill time?" We who have hobbies pity the people with this complaint. We believe we are superior because we have spare time supports. But let us think back. In most cases we will remember that it was only luck that introduced us to our hobbies. Meeting a friend at the right time or reading an article that stirred our interest was our lucky break. When we realize how little stood between our collecting stamps and not collecting stamps, we really appreciate the breaks we have had.

We can, with a little effort, and a little going out of our way, help others to the same good fortune we have had. When we know someone is close to retirement we can show him the joys of stamp collecting. We can emphasize its values to collectors at all economic levels. Mixture box collectors or rarity buyers, topical collectors or one-country specialists, can all partake of the fun.

Spread the word: tell about the good things stamp collecting has in store for all its followers. You will be doing a good turn to those who listen and of course making your own collection more important for every convert that you gain.

* * *

There are thousands of varieties of stamps available today for no more and frequently for less than they sold for in 1920. The sixty years that have elapsed since then haven't made most of the common items of the first eighty years of stamps scarce. A packet of 1,000 different sold by Scott Stamp and Coin Company nearly seventy years ago for a couple dollars is still worth only a small sum.

What all this means is that scarce and valuable items do the increasing in price. Common stamps stay common, generation after generation. There are just too many of them.

On the other hand, the fun of collecting is equally good with all levels of stamps. If a collector can afford rare items and buys them, he is certainly justified by the pleasure and value he obtains. If he must limit his budget and collect only relatively common material, he can still get all the pleasures that our great hobby grants its followers.

* * *

Many collectors hope to make a profit from their philatelic activities. This is certainly a proper objective, but it is important to understand the economics of stamp collecting if one hopes to accomplish it. There are certain basic rules to follow. Here are a few of them:

1. Buy only the best quality.
2. Buy either used or unused sets, but not mixed sets.
3. While you must obtain common items in order to achieve completion, do not figure them in the value of your holdings. They are one of the expenses all collectors have.
4. Concentrate your purchases toward completing a particular philatelic classification.
5. Carefully store your collections, and provide full air conditioning when needed.
6. Plan to retain your stamps at least 10 years.

There are many other good rules to follow, but the above six cannot be ignored if you hope for financial gain from philately.

* * *

About thirty-five years ago stamp collecting entered into a fortuitous marriage. It took for a bride, "Topical Collecting." The first years for the young couple were almost a disaster because the groom's family considered the bride's folks to be inferior in breeding and totally lacking in respect for tradition. But, as often happens, they struggled through and, along with bearing an interesting flock of children including "First Day Cover," "Postal History," "Fine Arts Collectors," and a dozen others, the respectability of the now mother of many ceased to be questioned. The philatelic scene of today is a rich one with variety enough for all. The lonely couple of 1935 is surrounded by endless friends, each pursuing his own course of collecting. Very few eyebrows are ever raised these days at what would have been called strange behavior by our stamp predecessors of not too long ago.

* * *

Are you confused by all the sidelines of stamp collecting? Are you tempted to save every one you read about because they all sound attractive? Well, we all realize the difficulty of collecting everything in the thicket of stamp collecting activities, but where do we draw a line, how do we define what we will do?

I think that for permanence of interest there should be a definite link between the subject collected and you. If it is the choice of a country for specialization the result will be better if you or your ancestors have a tie with that country. A topic should be one that touches your keen interest as to subject, be it flowers, masonic, religion, sports or any of the hundreds of others that we recognize as being worthy of effort.

Then there is always the collecting of as many different varieties of the world as one can accumulate. This is a basic and inexhaustible phase of our hobby. Of course you will never complete such a project, but how else can you in a few seconds journey from Japan to Argentina, from Tahiti to Greenland or armchair your thoughts to any phase of the world's history.

Believe it or not, there are still more collectors enjoying worldwide collecting than any other kind, and, best of all, it is good for as many years as any of us will have here on earth.

* * *

The year that the United States Zeppelin set Scott #C13-15 was issued, that is, 1930, our firm started in business. For many of today's collectors that seems long ago, but in me it arouses an almost contemporary feeling.

My father and I started out in an office on the third floor of a center city building without an elevator. Along with stamps and covers we sold first editions and interesting Americana. Our first big sale was of an unusual Lincoln document.

Gradually stamps took over the entire enterprise, and by 1932, when we moved into a ground floor store, the book selling part of the business was gone.

Collectors frequently ask if we made much money on the Zeppelin issue. The answer is no. Dealers seldom tie up money in current issues beyond their immediate requirements. Capital is too valuable and certainly in 1930 a set of stamps costing $4.55 at the post office was clearly out of reach of most of us.

Shortly after the set was withdrawn by the Post Office Department the price went to $10. With fluctuation in between it is now around $3000. We could have made a great profit had we had foresight and the capital to tie up. But then when consideration is given to the hundreds of times we have turned over this money, I think that overall we have done quite well.

* * *

Perhaps some day, when the wealth of our country permits, we will be able to give each working person a full year's vacation every ten years. Because of the facts of job holding and economic responsibilities, few of us ever get time to consider what life is about. We are just too busy making deadlines, balancing our budgets and taking care of our normal obligations. If we are to get the full flavor of living and some understanding of our place in the scheme of things, we must have time to think about the universe, its wonders and the wonder that each of us is. We miss much that is enjoyable, we cannot comprehend the meaning of our relation to nature and we fail to establish our own relative importance because we are just too peroccupied for such thoughts. With the realization of my wish for a sabbatical for everyone there might arise a new brotherhood of man brought about by the greater understanding of our interdependence and the effect of all causes on all of us.

* * *

At the place where I am spending the winter months there is a ruined mansion. It is on the waterfront and years ago a Florida hurricane smashed it beyond reasonable repair. For these many years it has been a landmark sought out by artists for painting and by small boys for ghost play.

Its site is an island and is a place of beauty. There could be great joy for anyone who used it for a home. Boating, swimming and palm trees are at the doorstep. An unusually mild climate and restful quiet make it a place dreamers would love.

For many collectors, their stamps provide a retreat much as this house might for others. They enjoy the hobby and secure from it an escape from the day's cares. While at their albums, the weather is always fine, with no need to notice wind and rain.

Should something, perhaps not a hurricane but an occurrence in their lives, cause them to put away their albums nothing is lost. The years can pass. The albums are ever ready to resume the part they played in providing retreat from reality. There is always an opportunity to reopen them and once again to seek what they can so well give. This sequence is repeated thousands of times in the experience of untold numbers of people. If it applies to you, reach up in the closet, pull down a volume, and return to philately.

* * *

A recent article in the *New York Times* concerned a small country's objections to a stamp promoter's issuing a set of stamps for that country several months after their mutual contract had been teminated. There is no question that the promoter had a contract for previous issues and for the right to sell to the stamp world those items printed under the contract, even if many of them might never have been for sale in the country of alleged origin. The circulation of labels issued after the contract was terminated and alleging them to the official issues of the country certainly does no good for stamp collecting. Those who buy them for stamps are not always able to investigate their legitimacy, and government issued stamps they definitely are not.

I have heard objections that such information comes too late to be of help to new issue buyers. If that is so, perhaps we need a lapse of time before we spend our money to acquire the latest, a lapse that would give the stamp editors an opportunity to spread a word of warning concerning stamps that are really not stamps. As it is, everyone must be his own detective if he insists on rushing to market to buy as soon as he hears of a new issue. By waiting three months he might occasionally miss an item or pay a bit more, but he would not encourage loose methods of stamp promotion.

* * *

There is a commercial on the radio that recounts the bad events and dire news of our times. It then suggests the use of a certain medicine to pacify the nervous system and relax the tensions caused by all the distressing happenings. I have not tried the recommended cure but for 53 years I have had my own pet way to overcome tension and excess excitement. It is to turn to one of my hobbies.

When I open a stamp album, set a canvas on an easel, read an interesting book or write one of these short articles, I clear my mind of problems, trouble, distress and tightness. The diversion from the forced draught of commercial activity or family problems is complete within five minutes of turning to the hobby.

I really feel sorry for other people who have never found this relief. It is easy for them to say, "I don't go for those time-wasters," or, "How can you enjoy playing with little bits of paper?" They really believe that the total of our benefits is monetary and that is the only reason for developing side interests to our regular work.

We know better, however, and those of us who have found the marvelous tonic of having a good avocation are able to meet life's stresses from a strong position that might be summed up as contentment.

* * *

On December 2, 1953, we conducted our 102nd Public Auction. That was thirty years ago. I note from the catalog of the sale some interesting catalog values, for instance, the U.S. Scott #1—5¢ 1847 cataloged $32.50, the 10¢ #2—$80, the 5¢ 1851 #12—$80. To skip a bit, the 90¢ 1869 #122 cataloged $92.50; the $5 Columbian #245—$95 unused and the $2 1920 #547—$15. A sheet of #537, the 1919 Victory, was listed at $110, the 5¢ Pilgrim #550—a sheet $280, 5¢ Walloon #616 sheet $187.50 and 5¢ Lexington #619 sheet $112.50, the Norse 2¢ #620 sheet $60, 5¢ #621—$350. Then there was a set of Zepps #C13-15 cataloging at $135.

These few items will serve to show that stamp collecting has more than kept pace with today's inflation, for present catalog prices are generally way up from the above quotes. The same holds true down the line for better quality U.S. and foreign stamps. Of course collectors seldom obtain catalog price when they sell, but neither did they pay that much, since most items are sold at a discount.

Even with allowance for the change in purchasing power of Uncle Sam's greenbacks any stamp collector who purchased quality material during the 1950's is quite a bit ahead financially. It is just as likely that purchases made now will reflect as good a picture in the year 2000.

* * *

Present day stamp collectors have easily available a great many types of albums, mounts and literature to help them enjoy their hobby. It is not so many years ago that outside of three varieties of Scott albums, hinges and the standard catalog there was nothing. Now, if a collector wants to know more about almost any country philatelically, he can, through library exchange, get a study on the subject. If he wants a different type of album there are literally a hundred available. If hinges do not appeal to him there are countless other types of mounts.

There are even dozens of new countries for the collector who wants something different. It is no longer necessary to collect on a fixed pattern. Everyone can originate his own scheme. As a result we are bringing into our hobby many who formerly would have passed up philately. Now they are intrigued by the great diversity of what can be done. A woman might seek to gather, mount and write up all the styles of apparel shown on stamps, while her architect husband might be as interested in the forms that human dwellings take around the world as portrayed on stamps. The variety and plans of collecting are endless.

Yet with all this diversity there are still millions who conventionally enjoy the original type of collecting—one of each in its proper place by country and date. Stamp collecting is so great because it has what everyone is looking for.

* * *

In the course of our lives my wife and I have traveled the best part of a half million miles through the United States and Canada. An untold number of cities and towns that few tourists visit have been our homes for a day or two. There are less than a half-dozen larger places that we haven't visited. Everywhere we have found stamp collecting interest. It isn't limited to affluent suburbs or palatial townhouses. It exists and prospers as well in the industrial and rural sections.

Few of us ever stop to think of why philately is so widespread. We think only of our own liking of it and of the pleasure it gives us. If we live in a city with clubs and stamp stores available to help us in our collecting, we take them for granted. We might well be close by an auction dealer and thus able to inspect auction lots before bidding.

There are more than a million collectors without these facilities. They might during a lifetime of collecting never see an exhibition, visit a club or gaze upon a stamp store display. For them everything is done by mail—and yet some of the finest collections I have ever seen have been made by such people. A few of them have even displayed genius in their philately.

Consider yourself lucky if you are near other collectors and can visit with dealers; but if it is in you to be a great stamp collector you will be, even though the closest collector you know of can only be visited after a considerable journey. Stamp collecting is rewarding no matter where and under what difficulties it is pursued.

* * *

I once before wrote about a distant cousin who had just died at the age of fifty-two, leaving to his wife a large inheritance. But what of his life? He had worked 18 hours a day, seven days a week in his little grocery store. The was never any time for other things. Although as a boy he had the same brushes with art, literature, recreation and travel that I had, he abandoned all these and any other diversions in favor of work and saving money. It can be said that when he died he had not lived.

I am indeed thankful that my life has been different. It is enjoyable to look back on the travel, social contacts, work with social service organizations, adventures in writing and painting, etc., that I have enjoyed. Certainly some of the time used for these enterprises could have been devoted to my work and perhaps have made me wealthier. I have no regrets. My harvest has been a rich one.

There are few people in the United States today who will work excessively long hours. The use of the leisure we now have to achieve a broader life, one richer in pleasurable activities (including stamp collecting) is all to the good. And as the hours of labor lessen, let us continue to expand our enjoyment of life's wonders.

* * *

Life in America has changed a great deal in the past fifty years, but not always for the better. In 1957 I wrote the following: "The short walk to a nearby park for summer Sunday picnics is part of the pleasant memories of my generation. One member, who was delegated to reserve the tables and benches, arrived at the park as early as seven o'clock. The rest of the family came along about 10 a.m. There was always an afternoon ball game, a bounteous picnic supper in early evening followed by singing and perhaps a Sunday prayer for those so disposed. At the end of the long day, when the walk home seemed many miles to the tired children, there was a feeling of satisfaction with life and a closeness with the family that has been lost to many with today's motorized breaking up of close ties."

I would now like to add to the above the belief that collecting stamps on a family interest basis gives to those who do so the same kind of good feeling that we of an earlier generation gained from our picnics and various neighborhood activities such as block parties, election parades, street dances and hay rides. Believe me, it is worth trying.

* * *

I have yet to meet anyone who did not want the highest price obtainable when he sold his collection. This is a normal and understandable desire. But every once in a while I ask myself when dealing with those who are selling whether they have done their part to make a strong market possible when they sell.

Have they supported organized philately? Have they contributed what they have learned from their hobby to the fund of knowledge needed by future generations? When a local group arranges a show or philatelic event, have they done their share of work in the effort? Just what in their collecting career have they done to interest a fresh group of people in philately?

If the answers to these questions are negative, how can these collectors expect a line to be waiting to purchase their stamps when they reach the end of the trail? If never a new collector is made the old ones dying off will certainly decrease the number of collectors. If never a study group or collector's organization is supported then all collectors are open to the fraud these groups protect us from. I could go on and on about the subject but I am sure you have the idea. In essence it is, "give to get," a perhaps selfish but certainly rewarding approach to collecting.

* * *

There is a pouplar song that says "There is nothing like a dame." We stamp collectors can sing just as honestly, "There is nothing like stamp collecting." I cannot think of anything else in the entire spectrum of activities that presents the wide variety of approaches and procedures possible in philately. There is no interest of any human being that is not pictured or symbolized on stamps.

The basic desire of most of us to communicate with others of our kind is facilitated by stamps used to pay the charge for carrying messages. The lure of distant lands that we often cannot visit is partially satisfied by our possession of stamps from them. Our desire to better our economic status is gratified by the value of our stamps. Our studies are made easier by the knowledge gained from stamps. If we are so inclined we can study a single stamp, an issue, the issues of an era or a country or a group of countries for as long as we live without exhausting the possibilities for discovery of new information. We can enter exhibitions with our collections and, if we are deserving, earn valuable awards.

The list of what can be done in stamp collecting is endless. Best of all, you do not have to do anything you don't want to do. You can enjoy stamps exclusively in your own way. Truly, there is nothing like stamp collecting.

* * *

It is a long time since most stamps were sold at straight half "Scott." That bible of stamp collectors continues to be a fine catalog. Its indication of prices, now better understood than in former times, is subject to interpretation by the individual dealer. If he has a good knowledge of his business, its sources of supply, his operational overhead and expenses together with his profit requirements he departs from straight discounts to set up net selling prices that reflect his conclusions.

Thus we now have in the stamp business something that has disappeared from many lines—price competition. The factors of service, quality and terms that alone influence business in some lines also are important in stamp dealing, but with the price variations that we also have there is much reason for shopping.

My warning to stamp collectors is to consider the matter of quality above any of the other factors involved in price. Only by purchasing first class stamps can you form a fine collection. A price is not low or cheap when it is for the sale of inferior material. A bargain buy that turns out to be in need of apology isn't ever good value. Buy the best and have no regrets.

* * *

The valuation of a desirable stamp or cover involves much more than looking in the catalog or a price list for its price. Some of the factors to be considered are foreign to the thinking of many stamp collectors, but experienced professionals always consider them, although often subconsciously.

Examples of the factors are: How frequently have you seen similar items, is the shade unusual, what is peculiar about the postmark, is it likely that a further supply may come on the market, and how many prospects exist to purchase the piece? Of course, these criteria are not applied to a $5 Liberty or a current German stamp, and yet they can be required to value these same stamps when they are used unusually.

The choice of a stamp appraiser seems often to be made on the basis that he can read the standard catalog and tabulate totals. How far removed real appraising is from that is best exemplified by the impossible task of trying to sell all stamps at the same discount from catalog. Popular and unusual items would be grabbed in a hurry by informed collectors and the balance of the collection would remain unsold. Only long-experienced, studious professionals can properly value philatelic material.

* * *

For over two hours a boy about twelve and his grandfather past seventy sat at our counter enjoying the purchase of stamps. Their excitements were continuous as they acquired items for their collections started more than fifty years apart. The shade of a stamp, its cancellation, the difficulty of finding it—all these and many other matters made up their continual conversation. They were truly having a ball.

The younger generation is said to have become an enigma to us older people. We say we don't understand them and that they are unreasonable in manner, actions and desires. Yet here in our stamp shop we had proof that the separate generations can get together for hours on an equal and mutually enjoyable basis.

Stamp collecting isn't exactly as it was in 1910, but both 1910 and 1983 styles of collecting can be understood and enjoyed by widely different age groups. Philately is one activity that can and does engage all the generations. It doesn't require grandad to learn new tricks, nor does it require grandson to become an old fogy. Throughout America there are thousands of pairs of oldsters and youngsters closer together in understanding because of their mutual interest in stamp collecting. The passing of the baton from generation to generation is more loving and has greater sentimental qualities because of the intimacies engendered by our hobby.

* * *

Just before he was called on to speak at a dinner, a representative of the Philatelic Division of the Post Office Department asked me if it was known when the first postage stamp was issued. Obviously his position does not call for having such knowledge, since the philatelic end of the Post Office has to do only with current issues. This occurrance caused me to wonder how many collectors of current stamps exclusively could answer a simple quiz on the genesis of stamps. Perhaps their ignorance of the development of postal systems is as great as that of the Post Office employees.

It is important to know why the postage stamp was invented. It is exciting and interesting to know how mail communication was handled before 1840. The century and a quarter that has since elapsed is a second of time in history, but consider how the world has been made smaller for all of us because we can buy and use postage stamps anywhere on earth. Knowing something of this great story of progress is important to every collector.

* * *

A collector raises the ethical question of price in an unusual circumstance. There is a stamp known to exist in quite limited supply that merits a price of about $5. Some few dealer have by a connivance secured a limited number of them at a very low price and can temporarily offer the stamp as a premium lead for a token price. The question is: Should all the trade reduce the price of the item in question to the special price that is being used a either a loss leader or a come-on to secure approval customers?

It is my opinion that the price of the stamp should be maintained. The limited number in the hands of the promoters will soon be exhausted. Those who take advantage of the special offers will certainly then take advantage of the true scarcity of the stamp should they care to resell it. Just suppose the fellow down the street cares to sell his 5¢ Norse-Americans for 50¢. Would you, knowing the true worth of the item to be $25.00 or more, sell yours for his price? The answer is obvious. Each merchant sets his price on the basis of his knowledge of the market. He would soon go broke if he attempted to compete with every loss leader or distress sale. However, long after the distress sale, he is still around to serve his customers if he runs his business in a shipshape manner.

* * *

There seems to be more mental illness in our country than ever before. This despite a standard of living that is the highest ever known. Some may say that we always have had the problem but did not recognize it, and this may be correct. But the stress of present day life is certainly greater than that which our fore-fathers bore.

There is infinite need for the forms of diversion and relaxation that are leisurely, complacent and readily available. Not too many of our accepted pastimes meet these requirements. Stamp collecting is selected by many professional people because it is the one hobby that can slow them down. It is a sort of peace conference with their emotions. And, best of all, it is always within reach, because an album of stamps can be kept in any desk drawer for the solitary unwinding needed at frequent intervals.

Recommend stamp collecting to your friends who are forever seeking that which you have found in philately. They will be glad you did.

* * *

If I were asked to describe in one word what stamp collecting is about I would choose the word curiosity. By nature some people are never satisfied with what they know. They are impelled to seek information, facts and meanings beyond the requirements of their position. To them stamp collecting is an avenue to endless knowledge. The shape of the world's affairs for thousands of years is pictured in the stamps of the nations. The customs of the people, the beauties of nature and even the depths of the universe are unfolded in our albums. Indeed, there is nothing known to life that cannot be found pictured on stamps. Thus they are bountiful means of gratifying man's curiosity.

Beyond that, however, it may be asked, "What that is beneficial does he do with the learning he has acquired from philately? Does the stamp collector become more tolerant, more discerning in his opinions? Is he, because he knows more, better able to make advantageous decisions in his own life? Are his tastes improved by familiarity with the customs of others?"

Every individual who collects stamps can sit in solitary judgment in answering the above. I hope that most of us reach an affirmative conclusion.

* * *

I have seen stamp collections that include the most unusual and rare material and yet are eyesores. On the other hand, I have gazed with untold admiration on common stamps tastefully arranged and beautifully presented. It is probably hopeless to expect that because one is a stamp collector he also possesses the attributes of neatness, art appreciation and system. We recruit to our ranks many without such qualities.

Even so, when a collector uses mounts other than hinges and permits his pages to be examples of slipping, crooked, crowded work, often times made worse by a contrast of black background, I am tempted to give him my frank opinion. And that is that his stamps deserve better of him.

Take a look at your albums. If you were the art instructor at the local high school would you use them as examples of a stamp collection beautifully presented? If the answer is no, why not try to improve on what you have, not necessarily for exhibition purposes, but for your own pleasure? It is worth a try.

* * *

Lady Bird Johnson had a grand idea: Let us beautify America. And most certainly we have much to beautify. Our cities are frequently ugly, without planning, choice building material or architectural taste. The small towns are certainly no better and often worse.

The exceptions to the above are so few that they stand out. Some large cities such as Pittsburgh and Philadelphia have successfully beautified parts of their area. Many New England towns and their counterparts as far west as Iowa are lovely, particularly if laid out around commons or a central square.

To return to Philadelphia; there is probably no more beautiful avenue in America than its Benjamin Franklin Parkway. This wide, tree-lined boulevard was started in 1911. It eradicated many old and run-down blocks of houses and service buildings. In their place are handsome structures, every one approved by the city art commission before being built. Another good Philadelphia rule is to limit the heights of buildings. Traffic congestion is only made worse if builders can join the sky-reaching derby without restriction.

But this is not a column to glorify my native city—of which I am very proud. It is to suggest a long series of postage stamps, each value to depict one of the beauty spots of our cities. Perhaps by this means we could stimulate a belief that it is a right of the people to insist that their town be made more beautiful. The Philadelphia Art Commission should have a counterpart everywhere. If they could legally turn thumbs down on plans that didn't improve our cities, those who build would be forced to consider appearance as well as utility.

* * *

Cover collecting takes many directions. It includes the gathering of material issued over a period of more than five centuries. The rare and valuable messages of medieval churchmen, aristrocracy and business are collectable covers just as are recent issues of philatelically made cacheted covers. Those whose inclinations are toward cover collecting can choose their field.

To me a cover is desirable if it adds to the information conveyed by the stamp. Otherwise I would just as soon have only the stamp. Such things as interesting messages enclosed, clear and desirable postmarks, advertising on the envelope, an unusual route, a rare rate, a historic connection and probably many others make covers attractive to me.

I have been over large correspondences in which only a few covers had philatelic appeal. On the other hand, there have been times when every envelope and folder letter deserved to be treasured.

* * *

In the course of my lifetime, by reason of the inventiveness of man, life in America has completely changed. The city streets with only an occasional auto, a few bicycles, many horse-drawn vehicles, changed during my boyhood. School buses were unknown and a five-mile walk to high school (to save the 7½¢ trolley fare for fun on the weekend) was a natural part of being educated. The wonders of electricity, an accepted service to today's children, didn't become part of our household until I was halfway through grade school. The telephone came to us even later, and it was a long time before I conquered my apprehension of it and used it freely.

Stamp collecting has changed also. Philately was introduced to me on a 10¢-a-week allowance. The general collection of my youth was almost the only type known. Scott's was a virtual monopoly in 1910. Mekeel's was the only stamp journal of national distribution at that time.

Now there have been many changes. Children come to us with $20 and even $50 bills to spend on their stamps. Almost everyone has a specialty or specialties. There are many competitive album and catalog publishers, and half a dozen national stamp journals.

Through all this time, with all the amazing improvements for living, with the exciting history, to me stamp collecting has remained the best and greatest hobby.

* * *

For some of its followers stamp collecting is confined solely to getting the latest stamps as soon as possible. They try to keep up to date in the areas that they are saving. I am sure that to such collectors there is much enjoyment in "post office patronage," but I would like to direct their attention to the enormous part of philately they are neglecting.

The scarce and desirable stamps of the past were all new issues at one time and possess every quality of exictement of the latest stamp out. In addition, the older stamps have a history of their own, and there is usually some degree of difficulty in obtaining them. This adds to the thrill of the chase. While it isn't necessarily so, the price of earlier items may include a payment for scarcity, but such stamps are the type to seek if one hopes for future increase in the value of his holdings. A stamp that has already demonstrated price increase when you buy it is more likely to continue in that direction than the majority of new issues that glut the market for years after their appearance.

The great fascination of working toward completion necessitates seeking earlier issues. And, best of all, at the present cost of keeping up to date, the collecting of older stamps is frequently less expensive.

* * *

I met a lady who heard that postage due stamps were to be discontinued in the United States, whereupon she bought 25 plate number blocks of the $5 value of the current set. I am no reader of the future but, based on the number of collectors that I know who collect U.S. postage dues in plate number blocks, she will have a long wait to recover her investment, let alone a profit.

I attempted without success to explain to her that stamp collecting wasn't what she was doing; that with the same expenditure she could have acquired much excellent collectable material that could be used toward forming a well-rounded and fascinating presentation of one of the myriad accepted stamp collecting fields. It is really deplorable that so much of the publicity that stamp collecting receives in newspapers and magazines fails to bring out the great pleasures of our hobby—the relaxation, learning and creativity that we all enjoy from our pursuit of the bits of paper. A mere saver of stamps is missing our purpose. It's fine to make a gain from stamps, but if that were all we could obtain from them our hobby would die overnight.

* * *

I readily concede that the stamps of Latin America aren't the world's most popular. The more economically advanced countries of Western Europe, North America, and exceptional countries such as Japan are preferred by many stamp collectors, as they do show the greater advances in catalog value from year to year. But there are other important qualities than catalog value. There is the story in back of the stamp, the history of the government that issued it, its availability, its cost compared to rarity; where the stamp stands in measure of philatelic worth. On all these points, Latin America scores well.

The great cultures of the Incas, Aztecs, and Toltecs, compare favorably in any contrast with ancient civilizations from other parts of the world. Constitutional government in Latin America has been quite volatile, but certainly not dull. There are excellent stocks of Latin American stamps available. Many real rarities, items issued in very limited quantities, sell for a fraction of what they would bring if from Europe or the United States. Brazil is forging ahead at a great rate. Colombia is now a great nation. Given the balance of this century, the names Chile, Peru, Venezuela, and others will join this important list. Nickel and dime stamps will become dollar items as this progress gains momentum. Collectors will look back and wish they had put more effort on their Latin American albums.

* * *

I have a good friend who specializes in the stamps of China. That is a big enough field to absorb the leisure time of most collectors, but this man has added to it the saving of worldwide stamps with full town cancellations. He travels extensively and gets into stamp shops all over the world. If they don't have any China for him, they are sure to have some stamps of some country cancelled so that the post office of origin can be read in the cancellation on the stamp. Thus my friend is always able to get additions to his collection. His main goal is always China, but the other interest is broad enough to make possible entertainment from any stock of stamps.

Specialists who bewail that they cannot find anything to add to their collections (and there are many who have reached this advanced class) should consider adding a broad new collecting field, not necessarily one that is expensive, but one that once again returns them to the fold of stamp shoppers.

* * *

I never have been able to understand why some collectors and dealers enjoy being spoilsports. They are never happy except when they are trying to convert other collectors to change to their pet form of collecting. There are thousands of followers of our hobby who thoroughly enjoy general collecting. They get their fun from filling in the missing items in their albums. To them, it is relaxing, educational and a satisfactory way to pass leisure time—that is, until one of the wet blankets injects himself into the situation. He will insist that general collecting is a waste of time, money and ability—that the only thing that counts is the concentration a collector focuses on a limited area of philately. The belittler tells him to study, do research, become an authority, win prizes in shows. "Junk the general album so you won't look like a kid. Join the ranks of the leading philatelists; they all specialize!"

I say bunk to all this. Stamp collecting essentially is and must always remain a pleasant pastime. If you have found a form of collecting that satisfies you, stay with it. Don't let anyone spoil your sport. No one need be ashamed of enjoying himself; and if your enjoyment comes from filling spaces in a worldwide or area album, keep at it. At the end of the trail, you will have gained from stamp collecting its greatest reward, years of contentment.

* * *

The many "specialty groups" that have been formed during recent years are a fine addition to our great general stamp societies. The general societies are the voice of all collectors, and every collector should belong to and support them. They constructively advance the welfare of our hobby on a broad scale. By reason of their size they are a useful influence in promoting good public relations and in encouraging accomplishment in philately.

Specialty groups are small associations of collectors who are primarily interested in a limited phase of our hobby. The groups cover a wide range of subjects—from Polar Philately to Religion on stamps, to Australian Philately, to the Russian Study Group, etc., the entire spectrum of collecting is covered. These organizations are constantly working to add to the literature of their subject. They pursue with vigor matters that large national societies cannot consider, because the general welfare of collectors must be the prime consideration of a general organization.

No matter what your specialty, you should support its study group. The cost is low and the publications that they produce will be invaluable in increasing the pleasure of your collecting.

* * *

The automobile tourist who travels at high speed on our wonderful interstate highway system is missing all the touring pleasures except that of fast travel. The lure of the countryside, including small towns and villages, the variety of shops, houses, farm land and seeing people at work—all are detoured by most turnpikes. This has given rise to a type of travel called "shun-piking." A "shun-piker" uses the old roads, whenever possible, leisurely goes through forgotten towns, stopping at every interesting sight and enjoying to the fullest all the color, fragrance and beauty to be found in almost every countryside. Forty or fifty years ago, when that was the only kind of automobile travel possible, when speeds averaged twenty-five miles an hour and a two hundred mile trip was a long day's journey, we knew in detail the country we traversed. Now, all we say is that we stayed outside Philadelphia on Tuesday night and near Cleveland on Wednesday.

Stamp collecting is for many somewhat the same story as automobiling. Instead of the slow, detailed classification of every acquisition that our fathers and grandfathers insisted upon, there are many today in such a hurry that all they have time for is to cram their potential collection into envelopes and boxes while they rush about acquiring more material. The joy of slowly examining a stamp, determining just what it is and lovingly placing it in its proper place in the album is missed—and believe me that is real joy. Slow down in your travels and your stamp collecting. You will soon notice that you have been missing much.

* * *

There is no one I know who collects blocks of three, but that is what Mr. X has after following the advice given to him by a fellow collector. He was told that hinged stamps are worthless, so he went through his United States block collection and removed from every block the stamp that held them to the page by the hinge he had previously carefully used. The removed stamps he proceeded to use for postage.

This is but one example of the free advice that floats around the stamp world. I have heard that children are told to do all their buying in the United States Post Office, a way of collecting that isolates them from the vast educational opportunities of worldwide collecting. Some collectors are persuaded to spend more for albums than for the stamps that go into them. Collectors not yet ready for it are influenced to become specialists.

Perhaps the worst advice from the viewpoint of the growth of stamp collecting is to preach that only rare stamps have desirability.

Informed collectors know that every stamp has interest and usefulness to collectors. Certainly, rare items are nice to own, but millions of keen collectors cannot afford them. Telling these people that what they have is worthless because it lacks monetary value not only deflates their interest in philately, but is simply untrue.

Our purpose should be to expand the pleasure people get from their stamps. We should encourage collectors to read and study good books on stamp collecting and then make up their own minds about what and how they will collect.

* * *

A great period of popularity for the collecting of United States Revenue Stamps was the late 19th century. For a period of years there was more advertising of the Revenues than of the postage issues in most journals of stamp collecting.

These were the years when business and financial leaders were men who as youngsters had lived through or fought in the Civil War. The marvelous engraving on a wide variety of revenues issued between 1862-1881 made for an exceptionally attractive group of stamps that had personal historical significance to many people.

Revenues are still extensively collected, but most of our newer collectors are introduced to the hobby via current commemoratives. They don't discover the beauty and fascination of revenues at the beginning as did our grandfathers of 1890-1900.

Research in Revenues leads into study of tax laws that reflect political history. The stamps themselves are full of printing varieties and in most cases can be plated. Handstamped cancellations can be arranged to illustrate the history of various industries. For a few, who carry over into Revenues the equivalent of original cover collecting, there is the stamp on the original document. Give some thought to this phase of philately. You will like it.

* * *

One of the philatelic personalities of my youth was a gentleman named William H. Emmert. However, he was Uncle Billy to all who knew him and because he collected stamps actively for 68 years, his friends and acquaintances in our hobby were very numerous. Uncle Billy was very apt to offend collectors and dealers the first time he met them by saying, "Many of your stamps are dirty." What he meant was that they were cancelled, but because of his love for uncancelled stamps, he insisted, without intending to hurt anyone, that all that bore postmarks were dirty.

I will remember how affronted I was when he first made that remark to me. I closed the stockbook I was showing him and turned to another customer who, I hoped, would be more interested in the stamps I had for sale. But then I got to know Uncle Billy and I found him to be the one in our area most willing to give his time freely to any worthy philatelic project. He regularly took two afternoons a week from his business to speak to school stamp clubs. By his insistence on the need of care and discernment in making stamp purchases, he guided hundreds of new collectors into building worthwhile collections instead of the mixed bag that some would have accumulated.

The "clean" stamps that he added to his collection, some as early as 1880, turned out to be a source of wealth in his old age, for many of them were by then high valued rarities. Uncle Billy died about 1945. There are many collectors who still remember the good his guidance did them.

* * *

A few years ago an Australian oil company distributed as premiums several million packets of stamps. I have been told that there were, in all, 8 million of these attractive packages given out with purchases of gasoline. Of course, the stamps involved were all C.T.O.'s of Iron Curtain countries, since no other philatelic material is available in the quantities this venture required. The project was dropped when it was realized that no wider varieties could be included in the plan and recipients were only piling up duplicates.

But the job accomplished what Australian philately needed. It made people stamp conscious. Today, millions of Australians have their stamp albums and philatelic ambitions. Their keenest interest is in modern issues of the South Pacific, but quite a few of these relatively new stamp collectors will come to learn about and seek older and more seasoned material.

It is a great pleasure to be in any of the dozens of stamp stores in Australia and watch the constant stream of people of all ages come in for the latest issues and First Day Covers. It is reassuring to me that the giving away of millions of stamps by a nationwide chain of service stations could result in acquainting so vast a number of people with the pleasures of our hobby. It is even more heartening that so many of them continued to collect after the giveaway campaign ended.

* * *

I suggest that the United States, under its new post office organization, issue separate stamps for each of its overseas possessions. The plan should follow the arrangement with the United Nations that indemnifies the department for stamps used and turns back the profit from unused stamps for the benefit of the country of issue. As precedent, I cite the special issues that were produced for the Philippines, Cuba, Puerto Rico and Guam in the past. We should now have distinctive stamps for American Samoa, Guam, Micronesia, Puerto Rico and the Virgin Islands. All these places can well use the profit that would be made to develop tourist facilities, schools, roads and other useful projects. Most other nations have special stamps for their possessions and offshore units. Tourists like using distinctive stamps when they write home from "The Islands." I hope the response to this will be to call our Postal Service's attention to this worthy idea—an almost painless way of aiding the economies of these places.

* * *

The view from my room on New Year's Eve was of an awe-inspiring valley between snow covered peaks with New Zealand's famous Mt. Cook towering in the distance. There are few more beautiful places on earth.

As the dusk gathered, a man with whom I was conversing remarked, "The mountain is dying along with the year." How wrong he was! Neither years nor great mountains die. Man's measurement of time is artificial, a myth to hide his awareness that nature prevails. Mt. Cook has a personality that will remain, oblivious of such indications as minutes, hours, days, weeks and years. The period of time that we called 1970 will always be alive in the life that was created during that period and perpetuated in its posterity. The only death is that inflicted by man in his wild and uncontrolled activities. Nature goes on forever. Mountains and men, deer and eagles are all part of a scheme that is beautiful until we, supposedly the most civilized of creatures, desecrate it. We have only the power to alter and destroy. Our hope for the future rests in our control of that power.

* * *

The richness of life in the United States is in sharp contrast to most of the balance of the world. It has been said that we waste more than enough to sustain 250 million additional people. Our scratch pads are large and a few words written on a page disqualify a sheet of paper for further use. In other countries a piece of paper is only as large as required, whether for notations or wrapping a package.

Automobiles are valued for many years elsewhere. Our system of trading for the latest model is difficult for people of other lands to understand.

We knock down still useful buildings merely to construct more modern structures. We do everything on a scale other countries don't even dream of.

The success of our country is based on its wastefulness. Millions of jobs depend on chucking out the old and getting the new. The money each of us makes is the direct result of our planned obsolescence. Stamp collecting participates in this scheme of things. We change albums, styles of collecting, philatelic goals and stamp dealers with great frequency. The newest and most radical ideas of mounting and displaying stamps take hold only to be soon supplanted by another newer approach to the problem.

This is America, the country where many can indulge in stamp collecting and other luxuries because we have more wealth more evenly distributed to apply to hobbies than in any other country.

* * *

The idea of showing what collectors have accomplished with the time, study and money devoted to philately is really what exhibitions are all about. In a show a wide variety of displays is an indication of the strength of the basic rule, "Collect what you like." On the other hand, an exhibition that shows a preponderance of frames of just one kind of collection is apt to make visitors think of the old kids' game, "Follow the leader."

There is probably too much pressure on collectors to become specialists or to restrict the scope of their efforts. Many collectors enjoy worldwide or general collecting far more than they would specialization. They are ramblers who travel from country to country at will via their albums. The tiny details that arouse enthusiasm in some collectors are of no consequence to one who changes countries as he changes moods. All collectors want to learn the history and geographical details connected with their stamps, but some of them prefer to have a wide-ranging, once-over-lightly approach instead of the demanding study of intensive specialization. For my part, I say live and let live—philately should provide pleasure rather than one-upmanship.

* * *

There is a class of stamp collectors to whom we are all greatly indebted. I refer to the "workhorse" of the many hundreds of philatelic clubs and societies. The workhorse becomes the hard-working secretary or else volunteers to set up the frames in the annual show. If publicity is needed, he writes it and mails it. If restaurants and hotels must be seen and negotiated with to arrange for the club banquet, you know who does it: the workhorse, of course.

Often this overworked member is too busy with club chores to have time for enjoying his own collection. Frequently, he has been at it for so many years that the members of the club take him for granted.

Your club has one or more of these dependable laborers in the vineyard; unsung, unthanked and perhaps even unnoticed. The next time the club hands out prizes give some consideration to your workhorses. They deserve and will appreciate the thanks their fellow collectors offer them. It will never be enough to compensate them for their devotion.

* * *

I recently spent an hour with a collector who had, one by one, made a worldwide collection of 35,000 different relatively common stamps. The cost was well over $2,000. His potential recovery would be at the most 10% of his expenditure. Some readers might wonder why, and for them I'll repeat what I have often written. The sale of low-priced stamps can be conducted only on a huge mark-up basis when they are offered individually to retail purchasers. The cost of such merchandise can rarely be as much as one-third of the selling price. Higher priced stamps carry a proportionately decreasing mark-up, until when collectors buy stamps for hundreds or thousands, the dealer is happy to have a 20% gross mark-up.

It therefore follows that if you are primarily interested in monetary return, you should direct your expenditures as much as possible to better grade stamps. That is where the recovery is most likely to be good.

I might mention that my friend with the 35,000 different stamps agreed that he already had been well repaid by the fun and pleasure he received in forming his collection.

* * *

We have all been told that it is folly to save bits of paper just because they are postage stamps. The sarcastic remarks of some of those who have never experienced the thrill of stamp collecting are part of the repertoire of jokes of some comedians. We don't mind it because we realize they lack the imagination to comprehend our kind of game. We let them go their way, getting a laugh here and there so that the audience is willing to pay their charge.

I wonder if any of these jokers have ever found the missing item for a chain they were constructing; if they have ever enjoyed locating something bearing the date of their birthday even if it was fifty years ago, if they have in their wanderings come across many people who were interested in the things they cared for and as a result became really close friends. Do they know the experience of solving personal and business problems because knowledge learned from a hobby turned out to be really useful? Do they recover from their diversions any of the money they have spent? Are they better citizens, closer to their children and less likely to seek the divorce courts than are stamp collectors?

With these and other benefits in our wallets, let the jokesters have their laughs. We have the gains and our stamps, too.

* * *

In the course of any year I receive several letters asking how to become a successful stamp dealer. Always the writer is primarily interested in how much money can be made from selling stamps to collectors. Rarely does anyone ever write to tell me that he has something fresh and desirable to contribute to the hobby, hoping that as a dealer he will add to philately's enchantment for its followers. Perhaps it is the same with all occupations, and people enter them solely for gain. Or perhaps I'm a dreamer who is out of step in believing that success requires giving as well as receiving. You must contribute more than hours of work, more than some capital, more than willingness to wear a path to the bank with your profits. You must add to the level at which you enter an occupation some service or ideas or pleasures that were not there previously.

There are hundreds of new stamp dealers every year. Of these, maybe one or two will be around in the year 2000, and they will have contributed to philately—to its social and educational aspects in a fashion that made these dealers deserving of success.

* * *

Certain philatelic items are outstanding with respect to beauty or rarity or both. Alas, in describing them, most writers are unaware of the wide range of adjectives available for vivid presentation to the reading public. The late Arthur Pierce, who by profession was a writer, always had my admiration for his ability and willingness to use color and charm in his word pictures of stamps or covers. Such words as "lovely, charming, rose-like, enticing, delightful, gratifying, satisfying, enamoring and elegant" graced auction catalogs written by him. In their way, those catalogs were as readable as the fine histories of New Jersey that he wrote.

Of course, most of the people who write stamp descriptions are not hired for their writing ability so much as for their philatelic knowledge. It is unfair to expect them to paint word pictures that are both accurate and picturesque. Nevertheless, for those who read many auction catalogs and dealers' lists day in and day out, there would be considerable added attraction if the usual words used could be mixed with the unusual that are available. How lovely would be elegant and charming phrases gracing some of the lots that deserve them.

* * *

An unusually large number of Rotarians and other service club members collect stamps. Since these clubs draw their membership from the top level of every occupation, this is a pleasing commentary on who collects stamps. We are apt to namedrop when we can say that thousands of members of an international organization limited in membership to the outstanding people of each community are stamp collectors.

Service clubs such as Rotary, Kiwanis and Lions are all active in useful social work. They raise and spend enormous sums for scholarships, aid to cripples and the blind, public services and health care, etc. It is a compliment to describe a man as a member of one of these wonderful organizations. It marks him as being socially conscious of his obligations to his fellow man.

The interest of these people in stamp collecting is inspired by an interest in the world. Service club members are great travelers. They want to see how the world lives. They collect stamps because through their collection they can expand their knowledge of people everywhere. This is one way that service club members learn of the problems of the world and initiate projects to solve them.

* * *

Many years ago, I couldn't understand why collectors wanted to save plate number blocks. At that time, the margins of stamps seemed to me to be uninteresting waste paper. Needless to say, I have changed my opinion and now have a full understanding of the lure of the consecutive numbers, complete sets of position blocks—and their relative scarcity.

Through the years I had similar feelings and then changes of attitude about first day covers, souvenir sheets, plating, naval covers, and many other popular branches of our hobby. Age has brought to me understanding and tolerance that I didn't have in my youth, when I believed that straight single stamp collecting combined with occasional commercial covers of particular interest was all that any stamp collector could desire.

Almost every year now unveils a new phase of philately, and some of them at first glance seem far out. But past experience indicates that many of them will prosper and eventually take their places alongside plate number blocks, first day covers, souvenir sheets and the many others that during the last half century have made the grade to wide acceptance.

* * *

Every hobby has its periods of frustration. The composer, the author, the poet and the artist are all well acquainted with what to the hobbyist seems reason to give up the hobby. In fact, I can think of no pursuit of man that doesn't from time to time throw up barricades between him and his objectives. When a stamp collector reaches an impasse between himself and his goals, I suggest that he put the entire situation and problem aside for a month or two. Just forget the difficulty of finding the sidewise watermarks needed to progress further, or accumulating the high price for the missing few stamps. Allow the mind to grow fallow on something entirely different. You might even, with profit, turn to another hobby for a while.

Sooner or later, with a degree of composure and the anticipation of great pleasure, you will come back to the philatelic conundrum. You will then solve it and pass on the other joys of stamp collecting. The prime rule is, "Don't crush the pleasure out of stamps with the press of urgency." Life is long and time has a way of making possible that which today seems beyond hope.

* * *

Baseball is my favorite sport. It is a game where luck plays a large part. From the time the manager decides who's pitching right up to the last out, inches can determine the score. The position of a fielder, the pitcher's controlling the bounce of the ball, and the swing of the bat can be on your team's side or against you. If for you, your team wins; if against you, the other side drinks the champagne.

Everything, to some extent, seems like this. If you are in the right place at the right time you can acquire the stamps you seek or the sale you need to earn the money to buy them. With luck, you will marry happily for life, but you might have taken for a wife the other girl who turned out to be unsuitable for long wedlock.

The mistakes we could make can frighten even the most self-assured person. Could this be the reason some people never make a decision? The wisdom of the ages tells us that no matter how clever or lucky one is, in the course of time his right choices will be only half the story. His mistakes will be the other half.

These facts being so, get on with the game. Play to the very best of your ability. If you do, you will win your fair share of the time.

* * *

Really great collections are not formed through casual stamp collecting. They are the result of keen study, reading, research and perseverance far beyond the ordinary. They do not have to include rarities, although it helps to have them. They do, in their writeup, arrangement, and contents have to reflect their maker's complete grasp of the subject involved. Some parts of our hobby lend themselves more to the formation of a great collection than do others. The major countries, with their intricate and huge postal systems, offer more for in-depth study than do smaller countries. While one can in short order exhaust the possibilities of research into such countries as a Persian Gulf State, India or Iran can become a lifetime study.

Before selecting a specialty, consider such things as how much time and money you will have available. In the past, have you soon tired of concentrating on a project? After all, some people like to play golf one day and tennis the next, followed by bowling later in the week. There is nothing wrong in letting the other fellow specialize, but if you decide to go ahead, select a subject that fits within your budget and probable ability.

* * *

I don't know of any type of crystal ball that is better at foreseeing the future than an ordinary water tumbler would be. This is my way of saying that the future is and will always be an enigma. There are too many possibilities in every situation for any person to be sure of what is coming. Of course, some good guesses have been made, but the laws of chance allow for a few forecasts to come true now and then.

Why then do collectors of stamps fall for tip sheets? Probably because they like to gamble and believe that some tipster has information not generally available. It is reasonable to suppose, however, that anyone with real inside information would utilize it for his own benefit. If stamp X is believed underpriced by tipster Y, why wouldn't he buy quietly at the bargain level and have a stock to sell when the price goes up? As a matter of fact, that may be exactly what he does, and perhaps he releases his tip when he is ready to cash in on his accumulated purchases. Then all who rush to buy as a result of his advice are doing exactly the same as stock buyers who bail out holders on whispered or telegraphed "inside advice." Don't be a sucker. Buy your stamps because they are useful in your collection. Leave the tipster's advice for someone else.

* * *

If you have never attended the annual convention of one of the prominent national philatelic societies, you should do so. You will find a grand degree of fellowship among the members there. Some of them have been going regularly to the convention for half a century or more and look forward to it as the great event of the year.

The meetings are not all dull red tape and stodgy reports. They are enlivened by good lectures, useful information and the opportunity to grasp the hands of collectors interested in the same phase of the hobby that you are chasing. The exhibition, if properly studied, will likely save you from many mistakes that are common to collectors outside the realm of organized stamp collecting.

And then there is the bourse, an aggregation of many stamp dealers under one roof. Competition and the rules of the bourse committee usually keep prices and quality in line for all the dealers, and you can have great fun going from one to another seeking items for your collection.

You need not be a member to attend the convention of any stamp society, but the chances are that you will join before leaving for home.

* * *

There are widely varying degrees of interest in stamp collecting. I knew a lawyer who gave up a fine practice so that he could devote all his time to philately. Another man was fired from his position of superintendent of a large factory because his stamp collecting interfered with his job. There are many such cases.

On the other hand, we all know dozens of lukewarm savers of stamps who couldn't care less about such details as perforations, watermarks, printings and the dozen or more other details that most of us believe to be essential parts of the hobby. In between these extremes are millions of people enjoying, to the extent they choose, the pleasantries that come from stamp collecting. For some, their complete social life is built around stamp friends. For others, there is the thrill of correspondence with collectors from afar. There are those who regularly budget a fixed sum for weekly stamp shopping, and more than a few manage to be eternally in debt for stamps they just couldn't resist buying.

Followers of our hobby embrace all and every type of person and personality. We are a true cross section of mankind.

* * *

What do you think of a man who for over forty years was able to and did spend 50% of his income on his stamp collection? Do you feel envy? Do you think, as many people would, of the other things he might have done with the money? Judgment can, of course, never be made unless you know more of the circumstances. Let me tell you that no one was deprived by this man's collecting. He fulfilled to perfection all his civic requirements and did more than most people do for their families. To say that his love of stamps was excessive would be to deprecate the complete joy possible for some people from our hobby.

Similar dedication to a science or an industry has been a large part of the reason why mankind's horizons are expanding both as to knowledge and physical possessions. Philatelic knowledge is no different. It results from a dedication to dig out the facts. It results from a hope that more than the one involved in the research or collecting will benefit. The geniuses who first plated the 1851 issue of the United States, or who rewrote the history of the West on the basis of what they learned from Express Company mail, had the same kind of drive and ambition as the discoverer of penicillin. Yes, philately can be compared with any other branch of learning in the dedication of its keenest followers.

* * *

It is a matter of notice to stamp journalists whenever a prominent person or someone recently in the limelight becomes known also as a stamp collector. Considering the cultural possibilities of stamp collecting, I expect our hobby to appeal to and be followed by many leaders in social, governmental, educational and industrial circles. Stamp collecting in many of its phases is perfect for them. They, more than most people, require diversion and relaxation.

As nice as it is to have famous clients, the stamp trade has a bigger task: reaching people of modest means, limited education and narrow reading interests. They need stamps for the broadening of horizons that are necessary to gain a balanced philosophy of life. The average man can, through stamps, learn in a pleasant way more of what goes on in the world than he could otherwise, except perhaps by enrolling in a good college. Let us strive to bring to the masses our message: "Stamp collecting is good for everyone." The rich or learned or prominent can find that out without our assistance. The larger public probably cannot.

* * *

Men's styles have been slow to do what postage stamps have done in recent years: glamorize. The lovely colors, variety of shapes and imaginative topics of present day stamps are a complete revolution from the past. Are men's styles in dress going to follow? This morning I watched a men's fashion show, and I must confess that the bright colors, original eye-catching fabric designs, and tricky cuts of the garments appeal to me. I might even chance wearing some of them when they reach the clothing store I patronize.

It's good to have change. There is no reason why men should always appear to be on the way to a funeral. Combining the utility in clothes with eye appeal is, I believe, a step in the right direction—that is, taking some of women's flashiness for ourselves.

We like colorful stamps, women, homes, automobiles, etc. We will probably like the new men's look after the first shock wears off.

* * *

I have always contended that hard work was the essential of success. I still believe so, but in many cases luck has to be added. A case in point is a man I know who has a cattle ranch in Florida. The Disney organization decided to establish its park four miles from his ranch. You can guess what that did to the value of his acreage. Overnight he changed from a man in comfortable circumstances to a man of considerable wealth.

The collector of stamps who finds himself the possessor of items moving up fast in value is, of course, lucky, because the chances are he bought for enjoyment more than for financial appreciation. It does seem that most of us in the course of our lives touch "Lady Luck" a fair number of times. The choice of a good spouse, having fine children, working at a congenial job, enjoying good health—all these must have some element of luck connected with them, because many people seem to miss out on all of these things.

Personal effort will always be needed, but the smile of Lady Luck is a real favor of the gods.

* * *

It seems that when folks travel, they make note of the restaurants they visit. This one was good food/poor service, the next one was too expensive for what you got, last night's dinner was not served hot, and so on. You hear reports from everyone you meet at resorts or on the road. Of course, much of it can be attributed to the personal tastes of the individual, for what is hot food to one is only lukewarm to another. This brings us to the matter of accepting the reports of anyone on any subject. Those who review books, plays, art shows or night club entertainment are, as all of us are, biased away from pure objectivity.

In stamp collecting, it's the same story. John Doe, who is infatuated with United States Revenues, cannot, try as he may, pass judgment on Cape Triangles without the ideas gained from his Revenue collecting subconsciously affecting his opinion. In every case of stamp exhibition judging this is bound to be a factor. Awards won or not won must be appreciated in the light of this fact.

The review of a play attracts or scares away only those who won't judge for themselves. So, too, I say exhibit if you are convinced your collection is worth showing.

* * *

In an effort to be of assistance, many stamp clubs and societies have appointed committees to aid heirs of deceased members. This is an excellent idea, but there can be problems. There are many reasons why such efforts can fail. Most club members lack experience in stamp dealing. I have seen collections ruined by the handling that committees of amateurs gave them.

Of course, if a collection is a modest grouping of ordinary stamps, all in the low price range and collectively worth but a few dollars, almost anything realized for it is a gain for the heirs. On the other hand, when a collection includes rarities, specialized material, unusual covers, or important sections that the committee is not familiar with, any advice that they render is questionable. I once heard a committee advise a widow to sell a highly specialized collection of Ethiopia through society sales books. Fortunately, she didn't follow that advice, and the collection was sold in an auction for several thousand dollars.

In any business, an experienced professional can be of more assistance than any amateur group. He will know what is suitable for auction or what fits into a private treaty deal. He can tell the heirs within a few percentage points how much to expect as their net realization. There are in this country philatelic firms with the knowledge, experience and integrity to guide any heir or executor to the best realization of any stamp property. For over forty years, we have been one of the leading firms who render this service. You can call on us at any time for prompt help.

* * *

A collector told me that the value of his collection must include the time he has devoted to forming it, figured at three dollars per hour. Of course the price he places on his time is low in today's labor market, but I think he is confused when he plans to recoup as labor costs what should be figured pastime.

You are not paid for attending movies, reading the daily paper, sunning yourself on the beach, or taking your best girl for a walk. Only a few highly skilled golfers, tennis players and other athletes are paid for their efforts and, in truth, they are really entertainers, the same as actors. Stamp collecting is a diversion, a hobby, an entertainment, that for collectors must pay off in enjoyment. Otherwise, forget philately, because there are no stamp collectors who will earn $3 or any other amount per hour for collecting. What they can look forward to is in reality worth many times $3 an hour—the pleasure of having spent time doing one of the most rewarding things in life and immersing themselves completely in a constructive hobby.

* * *

Almost every collector has his favorite stamp. He may like it best because of an experience he had in acquiring it; or its color, artwork, design or historical significance may be the reason for the "affair of love." My favorite stamp is one that is little known to today's collectors, but in its day was much sought after by all lovers of beauty. It is one of the revenue stamps issued during the Civil War to facilitate collection of a tax on medicine. The denomination was two-cents and it is the Dalley's Horse Salve stamp, Scott RS73.

It is a large rectangle printed in a rich green color. The stamp bears a handsome engraving of a horse. It comes in three varieties of paper: so-called "old" which varies considerably in texture and thickness; silk, a fine-quality paper with silk threads visible on its surface; and pink, a softly tinted paper ranging from pale to deep shades. Each of these paper varieties cost about $50, and I believe that any interested collector would be happy to pay those prices for fine examples of this truly beautiful product of the engraver's art.

* * *

What sort of picture of stamp collecting does the world at large have?

Many people believe collectors care only about the value of stamps. This is a result of the sensationalism common in both the philatelic and lay press. News of stamps is only the glamor of selling a rarity for a high price, while we on the inside know that not one collector in a hundred is affected by any stamp that sells for over a hundred dollars. To outsiders, the only collections of importance have items worth hundreds or thousands of dollars.

There are non-collectors who consider us ridiculous for wasting our time playing with small bits of paper. They don't realize that every bit carries a message and any interested person can learn about art, communication, history, geography, color, and texture.

Outsiders have no realization of the great social pattern of philatelic organizations, providing many of us our greatest enjoyment in philately. Through our hobby we meet and associate, on a non-discriminating basis, with the rich and the poor, the professional and the blue-collar worker, and people of all ages, origins, and in all positions of society. The lone collector working away in his den, removed from contact with other collectors, is indeed a rarity, but how would the non-collector know this?

Every reader, from his own experiences, can add many other popular misconceptions. It is difficult to get the world to understand what we are about.

* * *

Man is probably the most protected of life forms. With the exception of attack from his fellow man, he is relatively safe and can protect himself from all other animals. He goes about bending and molding the earth to his will, generally without consideration for what he terms when in a generous mood, the lesser animals. The few of us who question some of his destructive actions are often considered screwballs or crackpots by the many people who seem to think that man's desires are the only ones worth consideration. The fish of the sea, the birds, and insects are accorded even fewer rights than land animals. Yet, if we pause to consider the matter, life as we know it would cease to exist if any of these groups were wiped out. The plan of nature that permits the entire range of living forms to exist is a fragile vine that can collapse if any part of it is withered. As man becomes more numerous and his life more complicated, he had better give close attention to the limitations of what he can safely do to change nature's scheme.

Come to think of it, our hobby is quite as fragile as nature. The joys that it yields are dependent on the exercise of restraint by government postal departments, the ethical standards of dealers and the willingness of collectors to devote some part of their activity to efforts that will insure a supply of future collectors.

Everything is life is dependent on everything else. Nothing stands of itself.

* * *

Almost all stamp collectors at some time during their collecting careers get the urge to become a dealer. Many try it for a while; a few succeed and continue dealing over a long period of time. Why do the great majority give it up after a brief fling?

There are all the problems of any other line of business. You have to acquire stock, process it, advertise, check credit, fill orders, adjust complaints, accept losses, keep records, meet tax payments, etc., etc. Generally speaking, this isn't what the collector had in mind when he longed to deal in stamps. He had hoped for a nice, genteel, easy-going source of making money. He didn't expect the problems of any department store. Alas, it's not to be. Every business suffers from the same difficulties and regulations. When they discover the facts, most neophyte dealers withdraw, glad to be collectors again. Only occasionally does one stick to it, join our ranks, and become accepted as a professional by all members of the trade.

* * *

Choose a stamp, any stamp. Write down eveything you can find out about it. This would include its color, paper, ink, design, perforation, intended use, age, scarcity, attractiveness, historical significance, and anything else that it brings to mind. You have by now probably filled a few sheets of paper with information, all about one stamp. Then consider the great volume of information possible if the same assemblage of facts were made for the 200,000 or so issued varieties of stamps. It would fill a library.

Certain stamps such as the one-and three-cent United States of 1851–57 and the two-cent brown of 1883 have been the subjects of multi-volume books. The interest in these stamps is always at a high level because of the fascinating information available about them. You can, on your own, pick a stamp and do a research job that will be your distinctive project; and who knows—it may develop into another manuscript that publishers will fight for.

* * *

The Rotarian, the monthly magazine of Rotary International, devoted its entire December issue to children. There are many pages of poetry and philosophy written by youngsters six to twelve years old. The contributions came from India, Australia, Korea, the United States, Colombia, and other countries. The degree of discernment, concern, and wisdom to be found in these writings is truly amazing.

This has caused me to wonder what the very youngest stamp collectors would contribute if a stamp magazine devoted an entire issue to their thoughts, art, and writings about our hobby. We might very well learn a great deal from such a venture. At any rate, we would get a view of stamp collecting that would be fresh and probably quite different from our adult concepts.

Few of us have ever asked the kids to tell us what they think of stamp collecting. Perhaps an editorial effort to assemble such opinions in a forum where thousands of us would read them could open up new vistas to our hobby.

* * *

Each year there are hundreds of proposals for special issues of commemoratives. Most of them are turned down by the authorities, and each time some group of people is disappointed. I wonder if an arrangement somewhat like that of the Civil War Match and Medicine stamps would be useful in this circumstance. Private companies had special stamps of their own design produced by the government printers. They used them to pay the then current taxes that called for the use of a revenue stamp on each package.

Those interested in a special stamp of restricted interest could, under a similar plan, pay the Postal Service reasonable charges to get their stamp printed. They could then put it into use in the locality that had interest in the subject. An almost similar arrangement has existed in the issuance of commemorative coins.

These stamps could be called regional or restricted issues and would gratify sectional demands. The charges for their production would make them profitable to the Postal Service. They would result in adding much variety and interest to the collecting of our stamps. If the stamps were limited to low values, it wouldn't be beyond the ability of anyone to add them to his collection. Thus the joy of getting their desired special stamp could be spread around to many more people.

* * *

I have acquired a bad habit. I put things away and forget where I put them. The result is a great waste of time looking in drawers, files, boxes, pockets and all the other likely places, none of which ever seem to yield the wanted object. This is because it always turns up in an unlikely place. There is no explaining this contrariness in things I look for. In all reasonableness, I know that they don't possess wills of their own and means of locomotion to move from where I think I put them to where I eventually find them. And each time it happens to me, I wonder if I am the only victim of such tricks.

It all started years ago, when I parked an automobile on the streets of Uniontown, Pennsylvania. A few hours later, it wasn't where I thought I left it nor was it at any other spot that bore a resemblance to my first choice. Eventually, it turned up with the same amount of gas in the tank and mileage on the odometer that it should have, but the place I found it was over a mile from where my memory said it should be. From that modest beginning, I have progressed to where I search for my glasses two or three times a day, my pillbox seems to have wings or springs to change its location, the magazine with the article that I intended to read later in the day turns out to be another publication that somehow lifted the piece and added it to a strange table of contents; and so it goes, in all but one thing. Ask me where a stamp or cover is, and I'll lead you right to it. They as yet haven't sought to trick me.

* * *

There was a time, long ago, when most stamp dealing was done in single stamps. Collectors built their sets by acquiring, one by one, the items that made up the set. The advantage of this was that the collector always was looking for the missing items. It gave him incentive to shop around, because what couldn't be found with dealer A might be in the stock of dealer B. All this added to the joy of philately. It has often been said that 90% of the fun is in the search and only 10% in the possession. This has changed now, as has everything else, and stamps are advertised and offered in sets. You pay your money, get the complete set and place it in the album. There is only one time of hope, expectation and anticipation instead of the many that the buyers of singles used to enjoy. Perhaps this is progress; it may be more efficient, it might even be a better financial proposition, but if the essence of a hobby is excitement, anticipation, hope, desire and all the other pleasurable sensations, stamp dealers have reduced their frequency by modernizing merchandising.

* * *

While flying from Paris to Tel Aviv I engaged my adjoining seat passenger in conversation. He was a Nepalese from Katmandu and most interesting. Imagine my surprise when he mentioned the name of the only other citizen of the country that I have ever known. They were friends.

Back before 1941 I had done a good bit of business with the other gentleman importing many early Nepal covers and stamps from him. At that time Nepal was still remote and covers from there quite unusual. Now, more than thirty years later, I learned that my old correspondent was well and still collecting stamps.

If it were possible to check out the people who have passed through your life you would probably find that most of them continue on with their life style. When that includes philately they will undoubtedly be collecting stamps throughout their life. Most people sell collections several times because they either temporarily tire of the hobby or need money, but almost all come back to it. Anything with such appeal to a large mass of people is a great bet for the future for both dealers and collectors.

* * *

The stamp business (and other hobby businesses) are in almost all cases small enterprises. Even the larger firms such as ours employ relatively few people by the standards of most industries.

In a business like stamp dealing it is possible to revert to the time when every man could be his own boss. Most people lived in rural areas and were farmers or served farmers. The blacksmith, the country storekeeper, the wheelwright and the buggy maker were independent and free of all the restrictions of company rules. They succeeded or failed depending on their personal industry, skill and efforts.

It is certainly the same with stamp dealing. Success is a personal matter. Even those of us with employees can only accomplish our goals by making working for us both attractive and remunerative. There are no machines to sort stamps and arrange them for sale—only human beings.

After a long life I look upon the people caught up in mass industries with practically no say in their working lives and I am truly thankful that the dreams of a twelve-year old in 1917 were realized in my career.

* * *

The explosion of stamp collecting's interest in Japan has added a huge number to those who seek good philatelic material, which of course is always limited in supply. When a nation crosses the boundary of poverty into the land of surplus and gives education to its masses they become hungry for more than mere existence. They grasp for the earth's pleasures—travel, play, and collecting. Japan is an example of such progress.

It may appear that the Japanese in their new enthusiasm are bidding prices too high, but I think time will sustain their judgment. The indications are that in due course other nations will achieve wealth well distributed among their people plus education and desire to collect. Such countries as Taiwan, Brazil and Mexico are not too far from being able to support large groups of hobbyists. When they do, the supply of good stamps will be further divided among a greater number of collectors. I'll leave to you what the result will be.

For my part, I am sure that, barring a real cataclysm twenty years from now, top grade stamps will say to their owners, "Aren't you glad you bought me?"

* * *

You cannot retire completely. You will always have an interest in your former occupation and position. If this was in the leisure field, and that includes both collecting and sports, you will be able to sort of keep a hand in it while you relax in your retirement village. Even the man who worked on the production line will avidly read of changes in the procedures of his former factory.

Retired stamp dealers are particularly fortunate. They can, as they desire, take in stamp exhibitions and club meetings where they will be welcomed by old friends. It's nice to be able to keep up these acquaintances until the very end.

A different thing is maintaining interest in the new issues and fads of the hobby. I find that few retired dealers have any interest in issues beyond the time of their retirement. They seem to lock out of their minds the masses of material that daily comes on the market from many countries. For them it is enough to contemplate the current market and value of the stamps that they loved enough while they were active to have made a living from trading in them.

* * *

It is practically impossible for new collectors of today to experience the same kind of stamp collecting that was most popular in the early part of this century. The number of varieties issued by all the countries of the world was still small enough to have a space for each in only two albums. The usual collector of those days accepted a stamp for his collection in the condition he found it—either used or unused, centered or way off center, with or without gum, etc. As long as he could afford it, he bought it. Only a few who were far in advance of their time insisted on what we today call very fine quality.

Stamps were bought one by one; set buying was almost unknown. A completed set or album page was almost sure to have both used and unused stamps. A few United States collectors saved plate number strips of three. They were considered freakish by their fellow collectors. Sometimes many months went by between new issues of United States stamps, and then the new issue might be only a watermark or perforation change.

Stamp collecting prospered then as now and collectors of those days got happiness from philately the same as do those of the present. In that there has been no change.

* * *

We have medals and awards for collectors who achieve the particular results required to excel in stamp exhibition competition. The awards are many and varied, covering all phases of our hobby and providing incentive for all types of collectors to enter shows. We have completely overlooked, however, a group of people who have by example made stamp collecting a memorable part of living. I refer to those elderly people who can honestly boast that for as long as forty, fifty or sixty years they have been active collectors and added untold degrees of learning, pleasure and serenity to their lives. There are few activities of life that can and frequently do last as long as active interest and participation in philately. Shouldn't we recognize this and give a suitable award to collectors who can substantiate such a lifelong history of collecting?

Think of the honor that would devolve on all of us if it turned out that many thousands of our group could boast of a half-century or more of stamp collecting?

* * *

Many of us are called on from time to time to give talks about stamp collecting to groups of non-collectors. To some the invitation seems automatically to mean speaking about rarity and profit from philately. This is unquestionably an important part of the hobby, but I do wonder if it is the best way to convert the unknowing to our pleasure in stamps. In fact, the figures that are mentioned in many of these talks are more likely to frighten away some good prospects.

We should try to explain the wonderful therapeutic qualities of stamp collecting, the painless learning that all its followers gain, the social possibilities from membership in associations of stamp collectors, and perhaps in closing, mention that there is always a recovery value in a collection—something that few other hobbies offer. The recovery will vary with the quality and scope of the collection, but will always equal at least 100% or more if the pastime enjoyed is figured at a minimal cost per hour for the fun and the learning achieved.

* * *

It was a hot day and the big man was soaked with sweat. We were waiting for our cars to be brought out by the garage attendants. He spoke first and remarked that he wished he were not in a line of business that required heavy drinking because it made him perspire so much in the summer. My answer was that no job required heavy drinking of a person who didn't want to drink and all he needed to do was say "no thanks" when he didn't want another one.

This episode reminded me of stamp collectors who somewhere along in their collecting history have found a philatelic activity that gave them the greatest pleasure, but because of peer pressure in their stamp club, didn't pursue it. The other collectors in the club all chased something like extreme specialization or all collected British Empire or all followed a topical bent. So, belonging with the crowd was permitted to override the real purpose of a hobby—enjoyment. If you prefer not to drink, don't; if you prefer collecting worldwide in a printed album, do. It's your life and it's your privilege to do with it what you will so long as no one is harmed by your activities.

* * *

There is an amazing amount of ingenuity used in the creation of new issues. The forms, shapes, designs, colors, and textures of some recent stamps seem to point to their conception and execution originating far out in stellar space. Undoubtedly a small country is well served when, because of its exotic appearance, an issue of its stamps sells in large number to collectors in other countries. Foreign exchange, improved balance of payments, and painless taxation are considered worthy goals by all nations.

Many stamp collectors, for their part, feel joy at the possession of futuristically styled labels that are generally available for postage service in some country that the collector will never visit. Since one of the desired purposes of life is to gain joy, people should be happy if so little a thing as an issue of stamps brings the wanted result.

For my part, this joy results from delving into the historic issues of the past, but everyone should fish where he hopes to make the best catch.

* * *

I want to contrast two collectors I know. Both are rich, both are in their fifties and have collected all their lives. A thousand dollar price tag doesn't deter either one from buying. At this point, they part company.

One of my friends buys philatelic literature and keeps informed on the latest knowledge of his specialties. He has become a sound judge of the scarcity, quality and other fine points of everything in his field. If he were publicly known, he would be consulted by other collectors and perhaps be on one or more expert committees.

The other collector, an equally good friend, has yet to buy a philatelic book other than Scott's Catalogue. He says he collects stamps, not books. While most of his collection is first-rate because the dealers he patronizes are square shooters, he cannot tell you the slightest thing about his stamps other than their catalog number and value.

The holdings of each of these collectors would realize well in the six figures if sold; but for my part, I would much prefer the collection of the student. Its write-up is full of interesting learning that could be passed on to the next owner for his gratification.

* * *

Ever since about 1860 stamp collecting has been growing. The always increasing number of stamps seems to captivate an ever-increasing number of followers of the hobby. Seventy years ago, examples of all the world's stamps could be gathered in one modest album. Today the Scott Specialty series runs to more than thirty volumes, each in itself a great special area to collect. While practically every collector continues to maintain a worldwide collection, his major efforts are usually directed to some restricted group of stamps. This is because the size of the philatelic world has grown even more in scope than in number of collectors. Our grandfathers would have been amazed at the ideas of thematic collecting or first-day covers or plate number blocks and many other forms today's collectors enjoy. Advanced philately has succeeded in producing studies that are treasured by great libraries as basic to the learning of many disciplines. These often are far removed from less complicated collecting interests, but all methods and styles are equally important if our hobby is to give men and women great joy.

* * *

A surprising number of stamps with relatively low catalog values are scarce. Usually they are from the less popular countries and there isn't much demand for them. The collector who strives to complete a country such as Salvador, Paraguay or Zanzibar will run into the "little stickers" and maybe spend more time getting them than most of the balance of the collection. Informed dealers know of these difficult-to-obtain stamps. When they turn up, catalog value is meaningless because it will be a long time until the next one is seen.

If you have confidence in your dealer and he insists that ten times catalog is cheap for a certain number, you can be sure he knows what he is talking about. And you had better buy the item if you don't want to spend much more trying to find another.

In 98% of the listings, the catalog is within reason, but that two percent can be so far off that the fellow who threw the catalog out the window may have had a better idea.

* * *

My favorite set of United States regular postage stamps is the 1902 issue. From the viewpoint of engraving, design, portraiture and care of printing, this is to me the leading glory of our Bureau of Engraving. There are fourteen denominations ranging from one cent to five dollars and each one, when fresh and well-centered, is a pleasure to behold.

Some years ago it was my privilege to see a collection of this one issue specialized as to shades, plate positions and minor varieties. The owner also had many volumes of covers showing various usages, illustrations of advertisements, cancellations and private coils of the one-, two-, and five-cent denominations. He didn't have the very rare four-cent, of which there are only a few in existence. I think that all together there were twenty fat albums in the collection and it so impressed me that I have never forgotten it.

Many of today's collectors can do an equally fine job on one of our issues that appeals to them. The study of a single group of stamps—their usage and variety—is quite rewarding if pursued to a comprehensive goal.

* * *

We who are dedicated to stamp collecting are apt at times to become narrow in our tolerance of what we consider far-out methods of collecting. We should guard against such feelings. The directions that stamp collectors travel are entirely of their own choice. No one, not even an international exhibition gold medal winner, has either the right or the ability to say how anyone else should follow philately. The individual must decide what he chooses to do. If he favors boxes of loose stamps in preference to brilliantly written up albums, let us assume that his joy is in collecting in boxes. If he refuses to patronize organized philately, perhaps his decision is a wise one for him. If we ever reach a time when philately is a stereotyped procedure and all collectors follow the same path, our hobby will die of its own narrowness.

The hundreds of different collectors' clubs, study groups and specialists' societies are indications that many share the belief I express above. The individual collector who doesn't care for association should have the same freedom to go his own way that all these organizations have.

* * *

I wonder what percentage of the readers of stamp magazines are stamp collectors in the sense that the hobby was understood thirty or more years ago. How many of you have a definite plan to come as close as possible to the completion of your scheme of collecting? Does your horizon of philately lie in going to the post office for each new issue or in anxiously scanning incoming mail for your new issue shipment of last month? If so, you are much different from your dad or granddad. They made their prime interest the acquiring of stamps of the past. To fill in Austria from 1850 to 1930 was much more important than to acquire the newest Austrian issue. They worshipped Cape Triangles and British reds with their plate numbers, corner letters and occasional used-abroad postmarks. My first ambition as a collector was to acquire the number-one stamp of my favorite countries, not the latest issued item. I believe—and it was true—that the most recent item would be around later on, but the early ones might not. You who read this might sit down at your club and talk with older collectors about collecting in the early part of the century. They can really surprise you.

* * *

An old friend, long deceased, created a fictitious stamp-issuing country and devised all sorts of stories about its stamps. He called it

"Upper Darby" and he even wrote an article about plating its first issue. If you didn't know better, you might have tried to acquire a few of its stamps after listening to him expound on them or on reading one of his fascinating pieces about their details. It's a fact that almost all stamps possess the magic of those of "Upper Darby." The only difference is that most collectors fail to see the obvious. They overlook the possibility of study of detail that exists all through their collection and even in their duplicate file. There is something new to be learned about even the oldest stamp. All the previous study that has been expended on them hasn't exhausted the mine. If you have great imagination, you might be able to create your own "Upper Darby," but how much simpler it is to look deeper into what is already in your own albums.

* * *

I have just completed sorting and classifying a shoe-box full of Mexican stamps. It took me about thirty hours all told, and believe me, it was fun. I have always contended that Mexico is one of the greatest philatelic countries. There is probably no aspect of stamp varieties that she hasn't issued. The production ranges from the very crudest to the most beautiful. There are stamps worth less than two cents per hundred and others of great rarity. A collection and study of the controls printed on the early issues could take a lifetime.

In the box that I sorted, there were the usual number of second-quality items, but also many hundred fine copies. The highest-priced stamp found was cataloged at $80. The most interesting to discover was a five peso blue of the 1884 issue— a really scarce item.

Evey once in a while I take on the fun of this kind of sorting job. The next one in my plans is Venezuela. I have a huge old-time accumulation just aching to be completely arranged. On rainy or snowy weekends, when staying home is wise, I will be ever so thankful for stamp collecting and a reserve of material to work with.

* * *

A good friend and client has many times remarked that you cannot know much about stamps unless you have them to study. He will buy many examples of the same stamp so that he has a basis for comparing such things as shades, printing and paper varieties and cancellations.

He has been doing this for close to fifty years and, in addition to having a broad philatelic knowledge, has a wonderful and interesting collection.

There are those who prefer to collect one of a kind, properly place it in an album and then shop for the next major Scott number. But if ever the time comes when stamp collecting begins to lose its appeal to them, I recommend my friend's method as a fresh approach. In addition to never knowing what you will learn from the study of numerous varieties of the same stamp, there is always the chance that your knowlege will enable you to pick up a few sleepers from the unwary dealer.

* * *

The natural time periods suitable for sports are no longer recognized. Football, a cold weather sport, is played in August; basketball and hockey schedules seem to last nearly all year; baseball, with its too long 162-game season, would no doubt be more seasonable if the pennant rush started in May instead of April. Campers, skiers, skaters and all the others no longer respect what was once known as "the season"—that time when it was considered proper to play your sport.

Stamp collecting is no different from all the other pastimes. Dealers years ago closed their desks about June 15 and didn't resume operations until after Labor Day. Collectors put their albums in the closet when school closed and left them there until the brisk mornings indicated autumn was back. The single greatest impetus to all-year stamp collecting has been air conditioning. Controlled weather is necessary when handling stamps, especially if they have gum.

Football in August, baseball in March, ice hockey in July, and stamps all year around. How things have changed.

I have a good friend who must always be on the go. In his case, since money is no object, his being on the go involves flying to Vienna or Tokyo for a weekend and then for Wednesday and Thursday of the same week scooting down to Mexico City. A routine that would quickly wear out the average person seems to make him bloom. I envy him his energy but I'll bet he envies me my ability to find an interesting and exciting life right around home.

Just consider my avocations. I collect travel books, with an accent on Baedekers. I also collect United States Private Proprietary stamps together with the advertising cards put out by the companies that issued the stamps, and then there are Postal Reply Coupons, interesting Philadelphia View Cards, the Cubertias of Colombia, Campaign Ribbons and boxes of mixed stamps that need sorting. Together with my wife I collect unused patriotic envelopes of the Civil and Spanish Wars. Now you can understand why, while I like travel, I can be content at home. I have never run out of interesting things to do and don't expect to.

* * *

High school kids have problems we never knew in my day. Even if they are totally uninterested in college and would rather join the army than pursue their studies further, the parents insist that they struggle through the entrance exam requirements and apply to a range of schools. At about the time boys and girls were finishing high school fifty years ago Dad was figuring how much they would earn towards the family upkeep.

Then there is the matter of extracurricular activities. Art and dancing lessons, religious study and many other afternoon activities are on the schedule for today's youth. The school might have a camera or coin or stamp club that the kids would dearly enjoy, but the parents have already apportioned all the working hours. So if sixteen-year-olds drop their hobbies and sacrifice these joys of adolescence, it isn't by choice. It's forced on them.

Most kids are fine, decent, law-abiding and respectful. They want to do what is right. When we crowd them and take away the free time they long for we are making them rebellious. It is my belief that if Johnny or Mary wants to collect stamps, he or she can get as much from the hobby as from some pursuit they are forced into. And, if he or she is of a mind not to go to college, forcing that issue only creates another unhappy person.

* * *

As an eleven-year-old schoolboy I carried my stamp collection in my pants' pocket. It was a loose jumble of common stamps that certainly wasn't improved in condition by its home. A school teacher caught me looking over my prizes, and that is when I first learned of albums, condition and care of one's stamps. I am sure that anything I had in those beginning days wasn't of value, but no matter how ordinary one's collection is it should be well taken care of.

There are still collectors who subject their collections to heat and high humidity, keep them under too much pressure by stacking albums one on top of another, use cheap unsatisfactory hinges, use album paper that has injurious chemicals in it, and so on into a long list of things not to do.

Stamps are fragile and require care and attention. You should not toss the albums on a shelf in the closet and forget them. Aside from tempting a thief, they deserve better consideration. The money you have in your collection is oftentimes better than the stocks and bonds you have in your safe deposit box. Treat your collection for what it is—a worthy, desirable part of your life and your estate. Take care of it as you would a fine jewel collection. It is even more negotiable. Every care you put into it will be repaid by its greater value when you want to realize on it.

* * *

Certain pleasures can be enjoyed time after time without dulling the senses. An excellent speaker will always say something worth listening to and a fine operatic performance is ever a grace to its audience.

There are a few stamp clubs that one can visit at any meeting and be sure of a fine time. I won't list them here, but I believe those responsible for running these clubs should be coaxed to write their formulas, so that they could be circulated to all clubs.

The success of these clubs isn't only in the programs—it's in the art of executing the programs. It has nothing to do with the size of the club or its dues. It does have much to do with those who are elected to office and the committees appointed by the officers. A club that hasn't a single outstanding collector as a member can still be a fine club if it has good leadership.

Good leadership is the charm that brings members out regularly to meetings and makes them wait anxiously for the next one. It pervades the meeting hall as surely as would the fragrance of banks of roses around the walls.

* * *

I just took a ride in a 1940 Packard. It had only 28,000 miles on the odometer and in appearance looks brand new. Of course, the present owner has done some reconditioning work on it. When I compare it to the 1974 model cars I am most impressed by the solidity of construction of the Packard of 1940. The metal used was heavier gauge, the car seems to have a better contact with the road. Surprisingly, it rides as smoothly as today's luxury cars.

What does this have to do with stamps? Not much, except that many of today's collectors seem to believe that their predecessors of thirty to sixty years ago didn't know enough to form a first-rate collection properly annotated with the information that research brings out. Well, they are wrong. As long ago as 1880 some stamp collectors were doing more than hinging their possessions in albums. They were studying postmarks, rates, routes, printing methods and other details. It is a pleasure to see some of these old collections, both for their range and for the breadth of knowledge displayed. Good cars and good stamp collections aren't something new.

* * *

District 745 of Rotary, of which I am a member, is organizing a Collectors Club. All forms of Collecting are included—in fact one of the first members saves fossils. About half those who have signified interest collect stamps. This bears out my opinion that stamp collecting has as many followers as all other collecting hobbies combined. This includes antiques, old cars, buttons, campaign ribbons, coins and a list of others.

The sheer number of stamp collectors acts as an assurance for stability of value and a ready market for philatelic material. Millions are interested in stamps—the Postal Service estimates 15 million or more collectors in the United States alone.

Rotary has been honored by many countries with special issues of stamps. That in itself has brought many Rotarians around the world into our hobby. I remember the delight of Eugene Klein, one of the great dealers of the first decades of this century, when Austria issued an overprinted set of stamps in connection with the convention held in Vienna in 1931. If he could be with us today I can imagine his surprise at the present catalog value of that set which he sent as souvenirs to hundreds of his friends when he attended the convention. Surely, one of life's delights is recalling having received such a souvenir even if it wasn't retained for today's market.

* * *

Talk about being a stamp bug. I must be the biggest of all. Here I am on a vacation for the winter in Florida. All the pastimes of the "nothing to do" are available to me. And what do I desire most—a lot of stamps to classify. For fifty-eight years I have been either a collector or dealer in stamps. You would think that by now I would have had more than enough of the bits of paper that entertain us. You would suppose that one or more of golf, fishing, shuffleboard, chess, bridge, shelling, square dancing, pool socializing or some other diversion would entice me. They do, but not for long. I continually return to the original love. It's sort of as if a childhood sweetheart was always leaning on my shoulder.

Few things in life can be so long-lasting as love of philately. The games of childhood, the enthusiasms of the teen years and the delicious loves of early adulthood all pass into memory. None of these continues into later life. Stamp collecting with its magic stimulation of thought and imagination, is the exception. By no means does every collector maintain my degree of attachment through a lifetime, but enough collectors do for all of us to be aware of what this great hobby does for us. The thrill of the hunt for new varieties keeps us young. The order and art with which we arrange our collections keeps us precise in our worldly activities and the discoveries that result from our research send the blood coursing through veins that are younger for the experience.

* * *

During my many years of philatelic life I have met several unusual collectors. I don't mean unusual in the sense of what they have collected, but in their attitude to stamps. One of these men, a charming, well-educated individual, insisted on having at least two hours a day for his hobby. He always had a supply of ready-made collections in albums. He reversed the usual procedure. Wherein most of us seek to build a collection, his fun was in tearing it down. One by one he removed the stamps from their pages. After careful examination, so that he learned as much as possible about the design, perforation, water mark and cancellation, he proceeded to destroy each stamp. He said he was through with it and he was making the remaining supply in other collectors' hands more valuable. In reality he never had a stamp collection but always made sure he had stamps to study and destroy.

Another personality, a lady of means, collected by "orders from her daily newspaper." She sent off mail orders each day for selections of stamps from countries currently in the news. Her purchases of stamps would mount in direct proportion to the amount of space that Chile or China or any other country dominated the daily paper of her home town. A revolution or earthquake of severe proportions would cause her to seek even the rarities of a country. Eventually she had a huge worldwide collection, and it's pretty safe to say every stamp was purchased as a result of reading the morning paper. You no doubt have your own stimulus for buying stamps. If it's unusual I'd like to hear about it.

* * *

Let us consider an imaginary condition. Suppose collector A for twenty years has enjoyed our hobby, spending whatever he could afford on it and forming a better than usual collection, well mounted, including much better quality material. There have been times when the stamp money could have gone to another necessity, but love of stamps kept him ever faithful to the cause.

Now disaster strikes, a flood or fire destroys his home and he loses everything, including the stamps. With the exception of whatever recovery he can get from insurance he is wiped out. Let us consider his philatelic loss. Is it the full cost of the collection, its present worth, or is it a loss reduced by the hours and days of enjoyment that the stamps have given a collector? Suppose there is no insurance. Then while his position is pitiful, it nevertheless must be viewed with the value of all his past stamp joys as consideration. He has lost everything and, with or without the stamp collection, is wiped out. His other losses are only in some cases compensated for by past enjoyments, but his stamps may even have returned such joys, learning and social contacts that he has in reality a huge profit from them.

I doubt if I can sell this idea to anyone in the fix of Mr. A, but to me it is quite a reasonable judgment to place on the circumstance.

* * *

A collector showed me a cover that he was asking $16 for. In my estimation, a price of $3 would have been more nearly correct. When I told him so he said that a similar item in an auction had a suggested value of $18. He didn't know what it sold for.

There are a few things to consider here. First, did the auctioneer know the value of covers in this field of philately? Second, was he setting a sound value or inflating it to attract higher bids? Third, if it was sold, how much did it actually realize?

You can put any price that appeals to you on your merchandise, but if you want to do business, you had better base it on realism. Realism is supply and demand. In philately, such things as postmarks, shades, frequency of appearance, centering, freshness and eye appeal all count, but the basic value must be in the item.

I have known too many dealers and auctioneers for me to take their valuations without question. None of them knows everything. Few of them handle material from a wide collecting range. Probably the best that dealers can do on many occasions is to guess. After all, just how much time can they devote to studying covers from France or Britain or Spain or anywhere else that sell in the moderate price range? Therefore, when you read an auction catalog and are interested in a particular lot, find out what it actually sold for and not what an auctioneer hoped to sell it for. This is one of the reasons that we print prices realized for our public auctions.

* * *

A lady who saves stamps asked me to look over her collection and advise her if she was doing it right. There is no right way to collect; there is only the way you enjoy it most. After I explained this to the lady she still wanted me to look over her stamps in the hope that I could suggest improvements in her method. I expected to see a hodgepodge of philatelic material gathered without a plan and carelessly placed in albums that are quite unsuitable for the novice that she is. That is exactly what I found. Thousands of stamps, some expensive, nothing complete and all unattractive. The lady had a good time shopping for stamps but didn't have the slightest idea that if she strived for completion in some part of her collection she would be adding to the value of what she had and would also be opening up the possibility of having an exhibition entry should she ever desire to show in the local stamp exhibitions. Mind you, I am not suggesting that she spend more—only that she spend to a purpose. I also suggested that the importance of trying for system and beauty on the album page pays off in self-satisfaction. Carelessly mounted and unsightly stamps cannot raise a collector's self-esteem.

I haven't seen the lady since. I don't know if she took my suggestions, but to you who might have fallen into her careless collecting habits, do try to put some system into your philately. We all are pleased if we do a job well. Whatever your stamp collecting aims are, try to better achieve them.

* * *

When I was a small boy my greatest ambition was to own a Cape of Good Hope triangle. After considerable pleading, my father bought me one and I promptly either lost or misplaced it. I wasn't old enough to be entrusted with scarce varieties of stamps. Parents who rush their children into stamp collecting that is beyond their age make a mistake. The small fry are fascinated by variety, things from distant countries and attractive topicals. It sometimes takes years of this sort of collecting before they become ready for systematic philatelic acquisition and study. To insist on a child collecting as do most adults may result in them not collecting at all.

There are many adults who enjoy elementary collecting and are turned off at specialization of any kind. If that is their inclination I am all for leaving them alone. Don't try to change their philatelic style, because you just might terminate their philately.

There is room in our hobby for everyone who chooses to join us. There is a form of collecting in which they are most comfortable. Let each one enjoy the freedom of choice that we reserve for ourselves. It doesn't help anyone when we try to make rules that infringe on another's enjoyment of what he is doing.

* * *

During the early part of this century a bad habit was taken up by many stamp collectors. It was to write in pencil the catalog number and the then current value on the back of stamps. There may still be a few old-timers doing that, but most of today's collectors are too sophisticated to follow such a practice. Catalog numbers change, catalog prices change more frequently, and erasures of pencil marks can seldom be complete. While many of us accept the writing of former owners along with their poor hinging as part of the price we must pay for collecting the pre-1930 stamps, we don't like it. We all would prefer nice clean stamp backs. Those of you who are continuing the habit should stop. Surely if you cannot place a stamp in your albums unless it is classified in a detracting manner, you should do a little brushing up on how to catalog and identify your holdings. Let us all stop this unsightly, unproductive, undesirable habit.

Even the stamping of guarantees and O.K.s should be done sparingly. There are plenty of stamps circulating with false or imitative marks of accepted experts on their backs. Furthermore, some of the accepted experts of past generations have been discredited by later discoveries. An accompanying enlarged photograph of a stamp is probably better than an expert's mark for identifying and proving the item.

Those stamps that are marred by former collectors are acceptable, but now is the time to stop the practice for all time.

* * *

Somewhere there is a buyer for every stamp. The success of a dealer is in how well he matches his stock with collector's needs. A dealer could have 100 very fine U.S. number ones on hand, but if he doesn't know how to locate and properly show his holding to the right collectors, he could go broke for lack of cash flow. There is no such thing as a self-running business in stamps. Successful dealers must promote and compete as ardently as Sears, Roebuck does in the general merchandise field.

The amount of detail in dealing in stamps is probably greater than in most lines. Checking and classifying stock, advertising and distributing it, and all the usual chores of business, take great skill, patience and love of philately if the business is to be successful. The sale of an auto, house, set of furniture or cart of groceries is a simple matter compared with the arrangement and sale of shipment of stamps. In addition, most stamp dealers assume a far greater degree of responsibility in backing up their wares than merchants in other lines of business.

Most collectors realize and appreciate these facts. They cooperate fully with their dealers. The few who don't, who submit want lists for items they don't intend to buy or who delay making settlement for purchases, are soon found out and find it harder and harder to get the plums that all dealers have from time to time.

* * *

An old friend recently brought to us his stamp collection that he is compelled to sell because of financial pressures. It is beautiful. The write-up, arrangement and display of philatelic knowledge are superb. The albums are in perfect condition and the best the market offers. So what is the problem? My friend never acquired any of the scarce and expensive items in his specialties. He has all of the stamps most collectors easily acquire; none of those they must reach for. The collections will sell well and fast, but by no means for the kind of price you would expect for the amount of time, love and labor that has been devoted to them.

Of course, I know that most collectors cannot afford rarities and many are limited to only relatively common stamps by their personal monetary restrictions. However, it seems that a collector who has done as much study as my friend should have been able to use his great knowledge in the development of his collections and, on the way, have made a few discoveries that would enhance the value of his efforts. While important printing varieties, scarce postmarks and unusual usage on covers are always desirable, far too many collectors seek only the stamp and not the message. The message is what the stamp could tell as the story of its life. When properly told it takes the place of rarity and scarcity because it becomes a unique item as distinctive as the one cent British Guiana.

* * *

A friend just told me he expects to attend 24 stamp exhibitions in the next three months. He is a judge in some, an official of a few, and just an exhibitor or visitor of the others. There are 13 weeks in three months so he will come close to two shows a week. (I wonder what his employer thinks of this.) In my experience it takes several hours to view the exhibitions in the average show. Of course, you could run up and down the aisles in five minutes or less, but assuming that you attend for pleasure and learning, it will take time. Then there is the bourse that is often as interesting as the show itself.

Perhaps the lectures, awards dinners, and other side issues that every stamp show has do not interest my friend, but if he is to be a judge in several, he will be expected to take part in the banquets. I must say that in my opinion this collector is spreading himself too thin. He is attempting to participate in too much. He cannot possibly remember even a small percentage of what he sees if he looks at so much. He won't have the time needed to cultivate the friendships that grow warm on the exhibition floor. He will certainly not be able to avail himself of good buying opportunities offered by the dealers. He would be wise to visit fewer shows and he would see much more for his long-range enjoyment.

* * *

There are endless ways in which to enjoy stamp collecting. Every collector has his favorite. Mine is to withdraw to my den and, in quiet and solitude, sort a mixed lot of stamps. They don't have to include rarities or particular countries. About the only requirement is that there is a good number of varieties in the mixture. I break the lot down, first by country, then by issue, and finally by individual variety.

While I am doing this the problems of the world and my life recede into nothingness. If my body ached at the beginning, all pain disappears within no time. Soon there is a lovely glint in my eyes and even though I am physically at ease, my skin glows with health. There are few pleasures in life to compare with enjoying your favorite hobby in the way that is most appealing to you.

There will be some readers of this who would like to try my prescription but don't have an unsorted lot of stamps to enjoy. Let me suggest that they send for the catalog of our Public Auctions wherein are listed many such lots. Enter a few bids, or better yet, attend the sale if you can. Then, if you are successful, you can do as I do—have a gold mine to dig into whenever you have the time.

* * *

Millions of my fellow Americans are lovers of outdoor life. For some an annual trip to a country resort is the fulfillment of their year-long desires. Others more fortunate reside in small cities, towns or villages, and have rural living closer at hand. Perhaps some of these people don't realize the bounty that is right by where they live. We who travel long distances to camps and cottages in the woods, who revel in a lake or stream that even on the hottest day cools and refreshes are glad to pay the price of inconvenience in getting there for the privilege of being there.

I would like to suggest to the United States Postal Service a series of stamps to be issued over a period of years that would celebrate our great rural resorts other than the National Parks, which have already had their share of stamp issues. After all, Maine is more than Acadia National Park in the vacation and relaxation field. New Hampshire has much that we wish for beyond the view from Mount Washington. Vermont, New York and even little Rhode Island are largely rural and lovely resort centers. All through the Union to the great West and Alaska and Hawaii, vacation spots are important to the people and the economy. I would like to record a first vote to have some of these pictured on stamps. With the modern equipment now available they could be lovely reminders that we are still largely a rural country and want to continue that way.

* * *

Does your boss excuse you from work on the day your auction lots arrive from the XYZ Company's latest sale? If he realized how much adding those stamps to your collection means to you as compared with laboring in his vineyards he certainly would. Collectors react with varying degrees of emotion when they acquire items they have long sought. Some cannot wait to see a friend to talk about the event. Others delicately extract an item at a time from the package to extend the pleasure as long as possible. I knew a mid-western collector who from 1908 to 1950 never opened a shipment he received. His reason was that he was saving them all until he retired, when he could truly glory in his possessions. He had packages from all the famous dealers of this century, carefully stacked and unopened.

No one can say what methods or habits result in the most joy. For each person there are different approaches and results. My personal impatience that causes me to frequently rip a lovely cover in my anxiety to see the contents probably is representative of many sincere collectors. It doesn't really matter how you behave on the day your stamps arrive. What does matter is the care you have used in selecting your purchase and how much the acquisition improves or adds to the collection you are forming.

* * *

Can we compare stamps and stocks as investments? I don't think so. Here is why: Most stocks can be sold immediately either on the exchange or over the counter for a small commission. Stamps usually take longer to sell and carry either a higher commission or a large mark-up for retail merchandising costs. All the common shares of XYZ Company are of equal value. So, too, are all preferred issues bearing the same dividend and redemption terms. On the other hand, no two stamps are identical. The condition requirements of collectors being what they are, each stamp has its own value relative to every other stamp of the same issue. The wide variance can be as much as 99%, a remarkable range for any commodity. Some stocks have phenomenal rises and drops in selling price. This may be largely due to speculation but is just as often the result of special business conditions. Most better grade stamps have a gradual increase in value that takes years to become a substantial amount. In other words, stocks may be fast action; stamps are likely to be very slow.

For those who are content to wait ten, twenty or more years for results, the purchase of fine scarce stamps can be financially rewarding. Those who want to see a change in their investment value within weeks or months would do better to stick to stocks which can be sold short or held for a rise as the owner decides.

Stamps have the special advantage of being entertaining, informative and fully enjoyable over all the years you own them. If the value of these benefits is figured in, the stamp collector is almost certain to be ahead in the long run.

* * *

What do you do when a collector friend shows you one of his pride and joys, and you quickly detect a fault or the possibility of a counterfeit? Do you keep quiet, praise the item or frankly tell him what your superior knowledge reveals? This is a situation that every stamp dealer is faced with from time to time. No one enjoys disillusioning another but I have concluded that causing immediate pain is better than permitting ignorance to postpone the inevitable. The collector will sooner or later lose out in an exhibition or in trying to sell because of not knowing the truth about his stamp.

Yes, it is best to say, "Joe, did you have that stamp checked out by an expert committee when you bought it?" Or "Joe, I never buy items in this class without a certificate. Did you get one with it?"

There is no such thing as a perfect dealer who never makes mistakes. When you are spending your money for higher-priced items you are justified in seeking the opinion of students in the branch of philately that your purchases belong. Expert committees are made up of such students. The cost of their services is cheap in comparison with the loss involved if you acquire items that do not conform to what you thought you were buying.

* * *

The price you pay for a stamp includes the overhead and profit of the merchant who sold it to you. In general the higher the price of the stamp the smaller the percentage of the price that need be added to offset overhead. After all it costs about as much to handle a stamp that sells for 50¢ as $50.

Most dealers take a smaller mark up on high-priced items than cheaper material. While some common stamps have a wholesale value of as low as 10% of retail, some highly valued items may cost the dealer 90% of what they sell for. The collector who values his holdings without regard for these facts is fooling himself. The total catalog value is interesting to know, but it is more important to know what makes it up. One hundred thousand different cataloging $20,000 averages 20¢ a stamp, so can only be judged as a large lot of relatively common stamps. The labor of handling such a collection if it is to be sold by the stamps is enormous. On the other hand, 1,000 stamps cataloging $20,000 average $20 each and will yield a good margin for the dealer even if he pays a high percentage of the retail value.

Enjoy your stamps at whatever level you buy them, but be realistic about the amount you can realize for them. Every business must be concerned about capital investment, labor, rent, insurance, and profit margins.

* * *

Why does the Scott Catalog, a general listing, go into more detail with some countries than with others? If the perforation varieties of Norway, United States or Barbados are worthy of listing, then what is wrong with Austria? Why are the souvenir sheets of some countries accorded numbers and of others only footnotes? Why are shades of some stamps deemed important yet ignored in other stamps?

No doubt much of this has grown up through years of changing editors and owners, with the varied policies of each being incorporated into the system and with no uniform rules existing.

The Scott Catalog, for all its shortcomings, is a truly remarkable work. The scope of a worldwide catalog, the research and record keeping necessary to produce it are beyond the conception of any individual. In fact, the matters that I question could well come about because various portions have various editors who work independently.

When I talk to an active collector who states that he hasn't bought a Scott Catalog for several years I wonder how he manages. The learning incorporated in these volumes is a rare bargain that every collector should try to obtain at least every other year.

* * *

Every once in a while a collector tells me that he is giving up philately because of failing eyesight. Considering the wide opportunities of collecting it seems that even if a person is almost blind he can still enjoy some part of the hobby. Of course, searching for double transfers or minor perforation varieties would be out, but how about collecting advertising covers or all black or purple stamps? In fact, most of the topical classifications are easy on the eyes.

When you can no longer tell the difference in the size of grills you can probably classify the various fish stamps or sort sea shells from birds. I once knew a totally blind man who collected engraved stamps by the touch of his sensitive fingers. It was a remarkable feat but probably others could learn it.

The world of stamp collecting beckons to all. It has a niche into which you are sure to fit. Do not let some physical handicap cheat you of the fun of philately. Tailoring your collecting to your physical abilities is not alone sensible, it is rewarding in that you will be happy that your handicaps haven't deprived you of your pleasures.

* * *

There are many collectors who enjoy and form remarkable collections of Latin America. It is a fine field, full of problems for the student, beauty for the general collector and the opportunity to own real rarities at a fraction of their cost in other areas. Why, then, don't Latin American prices advance in line with Japan, Great Britain, Germany, Scandinavia, etc.? I believe the answer is education and income. So long as most Latin American countries lag in the schooling of their people, those people will have low earning power. Combine poor education with an empty pocketbook, and how can you hope for strong and widespread stamp collecting? It isn't possible.

Since the prime market for a country's stamps is usually within that country, Latin America suffers from weak home demand. This should not interfere with anyone enjoying the stamps of any of the countries south of the border. In fact, it will serve to keep them within the reach of a lot of collectors who cannot afford the prices the rest of the world is bringing at present.

Some day Latin America will stride into its own. In fact, parts of it are on their way now, and when that happens we will all awaken to how scarce many stamps from there really are.

* * *

The states are organizing. Within recent months both Pennsylvania and New Jersey have joined the ever increasing number of states that have organized societies to study their postal history. Some states, such as Michigan, Wisconsin, Oklahoma and California, have been the subject of study by organized groups for many years.

There is much to be learned in this form of group study. The history and development of all areas have close ties to postal history. The rise and fall of villages, towns and cities can be plotted by postal receipts. The story of the industries can be seen in the advertising on old envelopes. Main Street and grandfather come to life in collections of this sort.

We recently bought a large collection of Michigan Postal History. Though I never was a resident of that great state I thoroughly enjoyed several hours of examining the hundreds of covers in the collection. You don't even have to be a stamp collector to enjoy a nice cover collection, because there are so many things besides the stamps to view and study.

If you are looking for a new attitude towards philately, consider joining the group in your state who are studying its postal history. They will welcome you, and you will probably become an enthusiastic postal historian.

* * *

Everywhere you go in philatelic circles these days you see and hear talk about covers. They now sell at prices far beyond the conception of yesterday's collectors. Prizes in stamp exhibitions go in an ever increasing ratio to collections that are either all covers or well sprinkled with them. You seldom see an album these days that does not include examples of stamps used on envelopes. Why this change in collecting style?

Most stamps are available to any collector willing and able to pay the price. This is not so with covers, except the recent philatelically made sort. The supply of many stamps on the envelope as used is either miniscule or non-existent. This even applies to many stamps that are common off cover. In addition, the present study of postal history, with its look into routes, rates, postmarks, customs and styles of past times, in fact anything of interest that can be learned from a cover, has added many dimensions to the great hobby of stamp collecting.

I believe the collecting of covers will continue to expand. I believe that interesting fine covers of the past, including the pre-stamp period, will have a future value that will ever be growing.

* * *

I was recently with a group of people who, to my surprise, turned the conversation to collecting stamps. Frankly, I was completely lost in the morass of what they said. It seems that they all followed the Sunday newspaper listing of new United States stamps and joined the line at the post office on the day of issue to acquire a single, block or sheet, depending on their taste.

They conversed about current post office policy, projected stamps, quality of art and color—all concerning what was being done by the post office currently. My efforts to arouse their interest in something of the past fell on deaf ears. They spoke as though they were the inventors of stamp collecting, and all the catalogs, albums, handbooks, guides, etc., that have been the product of collectors for the past 134 years were of absolutely no consequence.

Rather than no collecting at all I am pleased that these people are post office patronizers, but I am saddened at the narrowness of their viewpoint of our hobby. I hope that before long someone will break through to them and open the door to a wider look at philately.

* * *

I am intrigued by the idea of creating a policy or philosophy for our country's future. Instead of a new platform drafted every four years by each political party we could have a long-term goal that everyone could strive toward. In a large sense the goal should be to achieve greater satisfaction from life in America. At a time when a third of our marriages end in divorce, when a large proportion of individuals and families are at the same time living well but on the brink of bankruptcy, when the cost of a modest house is four or more times the average family annual income, and when shortages and inflation hurt each of us, it is well to consider if a better or more pleasing life is possible.

I will not attempt to answer the matter here. But I will remind you that those who have a hobby have found a better life. The contentment, learning, and relaxation granted by a good hobby can be invaluable to any person in any station of life. High among the hobbies is stamp collecting. It caters to the love of arrangement, beauty, value and possession that is normal to most of us. When we measure our accomplishments we all include with pride the albums of philatelic material that are prime among whatever properties we call our own.

* * *

Can you imagine Archie Bunker collecting stamps? Well, I can't, because if he collected stamps he would no longer be the narrow-minded character he is. A stamp collector with only one eye sees more of the variety of life in the great creation called earth than do most non-collectors. They see a variety of cultures, customs, government forms, arts, beauty and aspirations.

The world of stamps is so filled with difference that it is virtually impossible to see it and be at the same time a member of the bigoted set.

Association with stamp collectors is a broadening experience because the hobby is so broad. In any club you will find a resource of knowledge beyond the conception of non-collectors. Not alone will it be the learning of stamps and their production. It will include expertise on all the arts, sciences, government and history.

Best of all, in most clubs a friendly discussion of any topic can be conducted without occasioning the rabid differences that are so disrupting elsewhere. I have yet to hear of a murder or serious fight in a stamp club. I have thousands of times heard that, "I learned it from the speaker at our club," or, "The speaker at our club aroused so much interest in the subject that I checked it out at the library."

* * *

It is difficult for the shoe store proprietor or furniture merchant to understand why the hobby business prospers in hard times. Shoes and furniture are purchased for their utility. Hobbies are a diversion and, as such, more needed when employment is slack than when overtime taxes everyone's strength. Few people enjoy just sitting. They want to do something while they sit. If it's stamps that they like they want fresh supplies to whet their enthusiasms. There are many people who will spend their last dollar for stamps who wouldn't think of cutting into their savings for rent money. Emotions and personal requirements differ but they cannot be denied.

Since 1930 I have lived through several recessions. Never have stamp sales fallen off until the return of boom times forced many people to desert their pleasures for longer hours of work.

During recession times stamp prices usually advance. This is contrary to every rule on the books of economists. This is an excellent reason to consider the philatelic contents of the closet that you seldom open anymore.

* * *

During the sunset of life there are many people who retain active minds but are restricted in their physical activity. Some of these are the fortunate ones who during earlier years cultivated a good hobby. To me a good hobby is one that can be enjoyed during rain or shine, while rich or poor, robust or crippled. The stamp collector has just such a hobby.

As long as one's eyesight holds out it is possible to follow the paths that philately pursues. It isn't necessary to acquire rarities, although if one can, I recommend it. Neither is it necessary to earn prizes in an exhibition, although if that is the goal, more power to you. All that is required for the full enjoyment of stamp collecting is a modicum of interest in the world about you. You then can select any subject, geographical unit or historic era and form a stamp collection illustrating it. It is fine if you are able to afford the expensive stamps that fit into your selected subject, but if you are limited to items that go for pennies you can still create quite a respectable showing.

Best of all, as life progresses and the body slows down you can until the very end enjoy this great hobby. I think that this is something to tell the world about.

* * *

A very well known philatelist of the early part of this century considered a pocket full of stamps the most important part of his day-to-day wardrobe. He was a salesman and frequently had to wait for his customers in the situation we used to refer to as "cooling your heels." Then he would take out his stamps and closely examine them for the printing flaws that can of course be found or imagined on every stamp.

Sometimes he carried really rare material in his pocket. I remember such things as sets of plate number blocks of the United States 1916 issue Scott #462–480. I wonder if anyone would chance the loss of such material in today's crime-ridden world.

The immediate reason for writing about this old-timer is that because of a storm I was bound to a motel room for a couple of days last winter. I would have given anything for a batch of stamps to play with. I don't, as did my old friend, make it a habit of carrying parts of my collection in my jacket pocket. There are too many people these days who will relieve you of anything so readily available.

This brings up another matter too big for me to solve, but sooner or later our society will have to get to it. This is how will we restore the sanctity of private and public property? How will we go about again raising all children so they will know the difference between honesty and dishonesty and respect the regulations that every civilized society has enacted?

When we accomplish this revival of morals and ethics stamp collectors will again be able to carry parts of their collections in their pockets.

* * *

I have decided that as a pastime fishing is not for me. Mind you I don't condemn all fishing, but the kind that fellow vacationers practised from the pier where I wintered in Clearwater Beach seems to be all patience and no fun. Hour after hour they baited hooks with shrimp, tossed their lines out and hauled in empty hooks. The wise fish ate the shrimp and didn't even touch the hooks.

Of course my friends got plenty of sunshine and fresh air but positively nothing for the table. If they depended on fish they caught for eating, all would have starved. Contrast this to stamp collecting. Whenever the spirit calls up a desire to philatelize a collector can materially add to his album. He can research some phase of his specialty or plan future purchases. Often he will have a supply of unclassified material waiting the deft touch of the tweezers. A stamp collector is never finished—every hour that he can spare for his hobby can be rewarding.

Then, too, the big fish that every fisherman hopes to hook is equaled by the finds that every stamp collector who has been at the hobby a few years is bound to make. As a last clincher of my opinion commercial fishermen consider their work difficult and dangerous. Stamp dealers love their work so much that they play with their personal collections in much of their spare time.

* * *

This has been a poor spring in the Philadelphia area. The cold weather has lasted right up to the start of May. High winds and heavy rain were frequent. If I didn't know otherwise I would think I was in Iceland. Indeed I have experienced better weather at times in Iceland.

Man does not as yet control the climate. He must endure what nature provides. However, all mankind is fortunate in that despite unpleasantness outdoors there are a myriad desirable and enjoyable pastimes available for the hours that must be spent indoors. Prominent among these is the collecting of stamps. No home is too small or crowded for a stamp collection. No location, be it in the Arctic or the Torrid Zone, is too remote for the pursuit of philately. No matter how rich or poor a person may be there are possibilities of collecting stamps. I have known collectors who could neither read nor write and of course many who had Ph.D. degrees. Among my stamp acquaintances have been missionaries in remote African villages, roustabouts in oil fields, seamen without a permanent address, sheepherders in rural Australia, men in the armed forces stationed in Antarctica, a botanist in the Galapagos, and rubber planters in the jungles of Malaya. It's a great hobby that can entertain such a wide spectrum of mankind.

* * *

For over three months I have enjoyed the glorious sunrises that occur almost every morning over Clearwater Bay. The change from black of night to crimson light and then the glory of day is to me a tonic. It gives me anticipation of another valuable day; one during which I will have a great share of happiness.

A neat stamp collection with its variety of designs, colors and shapes can do the same thing for you that the sunrise does for me. It can lift your spirits early in the day. Just try riffling the pages and drink in the fascination of your stamps. Few collectors permit themselves this pleasure before breakfast, but it's well worth a try. If you get the reaction that I believe you will, your smile will be broader, your handshake firmer and you will be a better person to be with for the entire day. And all it costs is a few minutes.

You might ask why I don't follow my own prescription and look at my stamps at 7 a.m. I frequently do when they are available, but here in my Florida home I don't have the safeguards necessary for their protection from loss. Next season I will be all set up and some of my stamp albums will be with me. Then I will have both the sunrise and the stamps. Am I not a lucky fellow!

* * *

There is no tomorrow for most of the things we delay doing. Somehow time contracts around day-to-day needs, and the trip we intended to take or the album we hoped to complete cannot be fitted into the schedule. Few of us possess both the means and the drive to do all that we hoped to do. So we compromise. We buy stamps, store them in the closet and wish for free time or retirement when, we resolved, we will properly classify them in our albums. It is sort of like the promise we make to visit Aunt Jenny each year. It's made in good faith, but somehow the expected free time doesn't show up.

All life is a compromise. Perhaps that's what nature intended when man was created. If so, and we accept that rule, there is still so much to living that we gladly accept life instead of its alternative. Nevertheless, with the addition of a bit of system and self-discipline, many of us can find the time needed for the activities we are at present postponing. Further analysis will indicate that the hot spark plug of desire is all we need. I hope each of you will find that spark plug and connect it to a wire labeled stamp collecting. If it causes you to arise at 6 a.m. instead of 7 a.m., or to pass up an hour at the tavern so that your collection is in better shape, I believe you will have gained a lasting pleasure. A sage once said, "We all find time for what we really want to do." May you really want to do stamp collecting.

* * *

There doesn't seem to be any way to convince "post office" collectors (those whose only stamp collecting consists of buying new issues at the post office) that they aren't on the path to riches. They have read about the inverted air mail selling for $45,000. They ask, "Wasn't that bought at the post office?" They say lightning that struck in that case can strike again. They give no consideration to the billions of transactions in between with no lightening strikes.

Stamp collecting of any type is fun and pleasant. It cannot help but add to your historical knowledge. It is better to be a "post office" collector than no collector at all. However, the deeper one gets into our hobby, the more one realizes that everyone isn't going to make a profit or strike it rich. A few will—but the many won't.

The many will have years of exciting joy sparked by stamps and their byways. What greater profit could there be? When you go to sleep at night after spending a couple of hours with your collection that has quieted down your nerves that are frazzled by a busy day, you are completely repaid the cost of that collection. To know some important facts that were revealed to you by philatelic activity is a profit beyond measure.

Look into the depth of our hobby. Choose some part of it that appeals to you. Remember, age isn't a factor that determines the cost of stamp collecting. Supplies of many early issues keep them well within the range of most pocketbooks. Let your collection be a reflection of you—an accomplishment of which you are proud. If possible, try to see that it is distinctive in arrangement and story telling.

* * *

Isn't it time to call a halt to the tons of garbage that are being unloaded on great numbers of collectors in the name of celebrating events of no consequence to the stamp-issuing country? Countries that would happily cut the throats of all Americans put out set after set of unnecessary pictorials honoring any happening their agents think will sell stamps. All they want is our dollars. Stamps—perforated, imperforate, souvenir sheets—pour into our country for the purpose of milking our unwary. Glamorous advertising aids this flood that millions of our citizens fall for.

There is a soundness required in the policy a country follows for the issuance of its postal paper if that country desires continued respect of the philatelic world. Far too many nations ignore this important fact. They even issue stamps for rates and services that don't exist within their borders.

Some few of us remember when a new stamp was an event of consequence. In the United States, there were years in which there wasn't a single new stamp. Now, I couldn't begin to keep up with the dozens of "Let's increase our post office income" pictorials. It's time to call this to a halt. Certainly, stamp collecting will be healthier if fewer governments try to milk collectors.

Publishers, collectors organizations and dealers must cooperate in this. We simply have to reduce the trick angles, the superfluous issues and the needless varieties. The question is, can we stop them in time to avert a crisis in our hobby?

* * *

Everyone knows the story of the boy who cried wolf. During my lifetime of stamp collecting and dealing, I have many times heard the cry of coming disaster. At various times it has been: too many new issues, too many high values, cancelled to order, poor service by the philatelic agency, albums and catalogs are too expensive, dealers are irresponsible, and on and on with very little of substance. Letters to the editor can start a crowd of worriers off on a new tangent.

And yet philately is today stronger than ever. I'm reminded of the calamity howlers on Wall Street. They shout that the end is coming and when their wail is loud enough the market turns and sets ever higher prices. Be assured that our world isn't coming apart. The strength of our hobby, resting as it does on millions of followers, is that of Gibraltar. In ten, twenty and fifty years philately will have developed beyond our fondest dreams. Small boys and elderly men will still be getting thrills from our bits of paper. Best of all, the value of those bits of paper will well keep pace with any changes in the purchasing power of money. Next time you hear, "wolf," act like a fox and bid in a few more stamps for your collection.

* * *

Somewhere today there is a lad or lassie who has just been introduced to stamp collecting. For the next few weeks the child's life will center around the excitement of acquiring more and more bits of paper for an album that usually is messed up. This is one of the most important times in the life of anyone. Properly directed, it can result in a lifetime of joy and learning. Neglected, it can be over within a month.

Parents or older siblings can encourage the young collector by a few words of guidance. If together they look up information on a country or the design of a stamp, much is accomplished. It gives the child faith in the importance of what is being done. Perhaps it will put order into a young life that until now has been careless. Never make stamp collecting appear easy. Keep it a bit on the level of a puzzle that requires skill to solve. Make junior feel that he has done a job well when he finds the right place for a stamp that has baffled him. Above all, don't flood him with too much too soon.

It may be in your hands to give the world another Ferrary or Roosevelt. Don't muff it.

* * *

The study of geography years ago meant learning about the 48 states—the names of their capitals, their boundaries and the dates of their admission to statehood. On a broader view the earth was studied by continents, countries, capitals and forms of government. As a result, every child was a storehouse of facts about the earth's subdivisions. Evidently the subject of geography as such is no longer taught to grade school students. Something called social studies has taken its place. The result is that the children know where bananas come from but have never heard of Honduras. I'll make the exception of those who are fortunate enough to collect stamps.

Why not a brief course in worldwide stamp collecting at about fifth grade level in every school? It could provide the kids with the knowledge that geography did in yesteryear and painlessly add a bit of worldwide history while doing it.

The cost would be minimal—small albums with maps and spaces for easy-to-get stamps, packets made up to conform to the albums and a package of peelable hinges. The result would be a real increase in the knowledge of the world's makeup, the kinds of people who inhabit it and a respect for people who have customs different from our own.

* * *

As often happens, a recent accident has turned out to be beneficial. I had taken the first stock book of our Cuba stock home to do a straightening job that stock books periodically require. I placed it on a shelf and my wife, Anne, in passing by knocked it to the floor. Alas, more than 5,000 stamps that had been sorted became a mixture, a mixture of considerable value that has required more than a week to re-sort. The benefit is that the stamps are now in a new stock book, which they needed. Poor stamps are eliminated and desirable cancels and varieties properly labeled.

Maintaining a stock of millions of stamps contained in about 1,000 stock books and numerous file drawers is a large task. We should have more help in the task but good stamp people seldom have the patience for this type of work. Strangely enough, I love it. I particularly like finding items that have been miscataloged, or previously unrecognized varieties. If forced to, I would probably be willing to pay for the privilege of such work.

My luck in life has been to be able at almost all times to do what I wanted to do. I wish that more people could be able to spend their lifetimes as pleasantly.

* * *

Few people know much about all parts of the earth. They mostly have limited interest in those places that they think don't affect their lives. Even those who travel usually have objectives that are circumscribed by their personal likes. Some favor seeing industry, others churches, and still others scenery.

Enter stamp collecting. The mere possession of a worldwide album is likely to arouse interest in places many people never hear of. Zambesia, Tannu Touva and Liechtenstein become more than strange-sounding combinations of letters. The album has spaces to fill for those countries, and those spaces call for particular stamps, each of which tells us something about the place. We may never acquire the stamps, but we are sure to glean some knowledge from the album. To us these places take on meaning. We soon know their size, population, degree of economic advancement, form of government and perhaps what they produce that we import and use. Then stamp collecting has done its job—it has caused us to expand our horizons. Our knowledge of Earth is broader. We are more interesting people because we know more and can place more facts about the world in their proper perspective.

Don't forget that the backbone of stamp collecting is a worldwide album, no matter how modest it may be.

* * *

A recent article in *Harpers* entitled "Boredom, The Most Prevalent American Disease" leads me to the thought that the reason some stamp collectors quit our hobby is because they are bored by the narrow confines of their philatelic activity. Collecting butterflies on stamps is fine for a short time, but after all that there is to know is learned about such stamps, the continuation of collecting them leads to ennui. Variety in collecting is the best antidote for boredom. Anyone who is interested in and collects a wide variety of stamps is never bored by the hobby. A person cannot exhaust the possibilities of a worldwide collection. Neither can British Empire, France and Colonies, Germany and States, Communist countries, or the stamps of the 19th century ever be complete either in having all the stamps or knowing all about them. On the other hand, a collection of Churchill stamps or Penny Reds is confining and often soon loses those with active minds. These specialties are fine if combined with other phases of philately to create a broad sphere of activity and interest. By themselves they wear out in a short time for most collectors. Old cover collecting is of course an endless game because of the possibilities of combinations of rates, postmarks, routes and other historic and philatelic angles. Choose what you collect with care, but don't so limit your sphere of interest that you soon go rocketing off your philatelic world.

* * *

I think it is very sad that millions of people have grown old with no plans for using their leisure time. Many of these people sit alone in their homes and, except for radio or television, only stare at their walls. They never cultivated the reading habit, find no purpose in sewing or knitting, aren't artistic enough to try painting or sculpting and aren't solvent enough to afford travel. On the average, most people can expect about ten yers of life after retirement These can be the happiest of all years but they must be planned for. Just letting all those days happen, letting them consist of the longest imaginable hours when you know they will be coming, is like the squirrel who didn't accumulate nuts.

Plan to have a good absorbing hobby for the late years of life. Adopt one that you can afford and read everything you can about it. Decide what you want as your goal in the hobby. Then, when the daily trip to the job is ended, you will be ready to start a new, completely absorbing daily journey, for that is what a good hobby is—a journey through the wonder, enjoyment and learning the hobby gives to you.

Of course, I recommend stamp collecting for your hobby, but no matter what you choose I hope it fills your expectations.

* * *

Some stamps are ugly. This may be occasioned by their designer, printing method used, or just a poor printing and perforating job. Often such stamps originated from countries that were technically backward in the early days of stamps. We must remember, however, that some of the earliest stamps are gems of design and production.

Ugly stamps can be as informative to study as the most beautiful. Indeed such issues as some of those of 19th century Spain are loaded with cancellation and plate varieties that would well justify a close study. There is a definite lack of appreciation of such study on the part of many newer collectors.

Groups of stamps such as Indian Native States, early Venezuela, the first issue of Persia, and some early Japan would never earn a beauty prize, but how absorbing they can be to those willing to trace their ramifications. The pretty pictures ground out by today's six color printing presses will never compare with the possibilities for research and creation of a topnotch collection that many ugly stamps afford.

* * *

Almost every collector would enjoy having a specialty on the level of the United States ten cent black 1847 issue. The stamp is well engraved, grand looking and popular. There is much that can be done with it because of its postal history association. These things being true, why is it that I don't recommend it to most collectors as a subject for specialization? The answer is it's too expensive. At $1000 and up, each, this is a game for rich people only.

When I am asked to recommend a corner of philately, my first question is, "How big is your stamp budget?" I must know the potential expenditure, because it is most necessary to induce the collector to choose a field that will show results for the money he can spend.

It takes a long time to build a truly worthwhile specialized collection. The unusual and difficult to find must be sought after. In many branches of philately, they are not necessarily expensive, but they don't rest in every dealer's stock awaiting your visit. If you have selected well, have patience, keep alert for opportunities, study all available knowledge and obtain ample material for your own study.

You too can, over a period of years, form a distinctive, desirable specialized collection.

* * *

While I was straightening up my den on a recent holiday I was reminded of an incident that took place several years ago. An old college professor had died in a small upstate town and his widow sent for me to take care of his stamp collection. When I got to the home, she took out a key and opened the door to his den. That was the first time she had entered that room in over forty years. She explained that the professor had threatened her with physical violence if she ever entered his stamp room. For the entire time it was never cleaned or put in order. You can imagine how thick the dust was on everything.

It took a day to pack the material and ship it to the office. There were loads of covers, mostly U.S. and foreign first days that were not at that time in much demand. The albums were nice and realized a fine return for the estate. The covers were offered in large lots. To our amazement they sold for many times our estimate. Years later I found out why. It seems several people, in looking at the cover lots before the auction, discovered that each sealed U.S. First Day Cover contained a plate number block of the stamp inside. This even extended to the high values and the #C18 Zeppelin stamp. The professor had ordered his covers that way and as soon as a few of our auction clients discovered the hidden value they resolved to try for a bargain.

The moral isn't to permit your wife to clean your den but for heaven's sake, stop hiding good stamps where they can be overlooked.

* * *

Not long ago I listened to an amazing story. It seems that in a small town a stamp collector died. The lawyer who handled the estate knew a collector and asked him to appraise the deceased collector's collection. The collection was a beautiful assemblage of the classic issues of St. Vincent—certainly a highly specialized field that few professionals would be capable of valuing. The collection appraiser knew U.S. plate blocks but nothing else. Nevertheless, he proceeded, with the aid of a Scott Catalog, to endeavor to establish a value for the lawyer. Some covers, worth in the trade several times catalog, were figured along with the early blocks and unusual cancellations at the flat rate of one-quarter Scott. The appraisal completed, the lawyer paid 5% of its total to the collector as a fair fee.

Suddenly getting cautious, he then phoned a well-known auction firm and arranged for an informal estimate of what the St. Vincent collection would realize at auction. The figure was more than three times the collector's appraisal. Eventually, when sold, it did better than that.

The lesson here is—if you want a surprise, always hire a plumber to do your carpentry.

* * *

It is Memorial Day or, as we frequently called it years ago, Decoration Day. During the early part of this century this was quite a holiday. Crowds turned out for the town parade to the cemetery where the formality of "shooting over the graves" was a solemn occasion. The community's leading citizen always had a fine speech to deliver. Invariably it included words about the superiority of America and Americans. When it was over we went home exhilarated, glad that our ancestors were men who loved freedom and personally resolved to carry on our fine traditions.

Now most of the above is changed. Few turn out for the ceremonies. Fewer still think about why we are having a holiday. Uppermost in many minds is how to combat the traffic that will cram every highway as millions strive to arrive home from usually useless automobile jaunts. Gone are memories of Grant, Lee, Scott, Dewey, and Pershing. What they stood for and impressed on our character is now taken for granted.

Along with our history stamp collecting is neglecting its traditions. For a century or more it was a leisurely joyful means to learning and diversion. Now it is becoming a mad race to keep up with far too many unneeded issues that come out so frequently as to restrict our ability to learn anything about them.

* * *

Who is to say that a fine collection of one country is superior to a great collection of another? Can we sensibly pit the United States against Italy or France? Each one has its rarities, frauds to be recognized and avoided, history to be entwined with philatelic write-up, questions of quality and all the other tough problems that the advanced philatelist must try to solve.

When in an average stamp exhibition it becomes necessary to choose the grand winner from among really choice collections, any decision made is likely to be unfair to the others. Aside from the frequent lack of knowledge that judges display, there is also in some places a tendency of favoritism towards one country or group of stamps. If the locality is heavy with collectors of British or Spanish stamps, you shouldn't be surprised if one of them receives the grand prize.

If I were in the position of owning a really outstanding collection of some offbeat country, I would carefully choose the exhibitions where I would enter it. I certainly wouldn't put it into an almost all United States show with much hope of success. There certainly are exceptions, but in such shows a United States collection generally comes out on top.

Many great collectors exhibit their collections for the good of the hobby. This is a noble thing to do and aids stamp shows to become more interesting. Everything possible should be done to reward them for their fine intentions.

* * *

I suppose there is no way that we can tell if a budding new stamp collector is going to become a great philatelist. The most avid newcomer to our hobby may prove to be a six-week wonder, while the dullest of interests in another person might suddenly bloom into an artist of some phase of our great hobby. I can think of many examples of each extreme.

To me the important matter is just what influenced some to quit after a short time and others to become more involved after a slow start. Often chance has a hand in the decision. A young man can fall in love and marry a woman who is so antagonistic to his pleasures that he gives them up. Another can stumble in a purely accidental way upon some valuable or otherwise interesting stamps that sway him from dilatory collecting habits. I recall that one prominent collector of today was so pleased at seeing his name in a newspaper stamp column shortly after he started the hobby that he has almost dedicated his whole life to philately.

Another friend who early in the game seemed to be headed towards fame as a research student of Mexican Postal History was diverted by that old bugaboo greed and wound up with a reputation that ruined any chance for his success.

Among the thousands whom I have known as beginners there lay buried some great stories of what happened. I wish I had the ability to elaborate them into real-life history.

* * *

I have been reading the biographies of United States Presidents after they left the Presidency. Almost all of them had financial difficulties. They had to spend their last years worrying about keeping solvent. How like our average citizen this is. The years of highest earnings seem to fly by and rarely is enough put away for the slide down the decreasing years.

Many people never earn surplus or have such heavy responsibilities that saving is not possible. Others make unwise investments or are swindled. Many of our past Presidents were in the latter group.

If, when a young person, you started a stamp collection, bought good quality stamps, systematically added to your albums and even through hard times continued the hobby, you have what is probably as good an insurance for old age as exists.

As long as you keep your stamps they will entertain you. Then, when the curtain falls, you will be leaving a property that is in demand and will bring an excellent return. Considering your years of joy this return will be 100% profit to your estate.

* * *

July 4th this year was part of a three-day weekend. You no doubt had your way of enjoying it—perhaps with a motor trip or sojourn at a resort. In Philadelphia almost 150,000 people went to the Phillies baseball games. I wonder how many stamp collectors used some of this summer holiday to do a few philatelic tasks.

We all have loose material awaiting classification and mounting. For those who could use a few extra dollars, the better duplicates could be mounted in society salesbooks and sent out to do a double duty—bring in some money and provide another collector with material he seeks. I have known many collectors who, while doing this job, have found overlooked items useful in their own collections. Every time you improve quality or add a variety, your collection becomes more desirable.

For my part, I did two pleasant philatelic things during the holiday. First, I visited a long-time friend who has been a devoted lifelong stamp collector. For several years he has been a shut-in, suffering from a crippling ailment. He lives about forty miles from me and every mile to his home and back was a joy thinking of the pleasure of our getting together to talk stamps.

The second philatelic happening was sorting a box of old Argentine stamps that had lain around the house for years. I haven't any particular interest in Argentina and have never collected its stamps other than the general collections I have formed. However, I must admit that I believe the stamps of Argentina up to the 1920 period as interesting and collectable as any issued by any country. At least the box I sorted made me feel that way.

* * *

Did you ever draw up a list of stamps you wanted to get, check what they would cost and then tear the list up? Almost every collector has done just this more than once. I call it tantalizing yourself. It's a form of punishment for not being rich. However, sometimes the tearing up need not happen.

Are you chasing stamps that seldom come along in excellent condition when your pocketbook could afford average quality? Do you insist on an all-unused collection when some of the scarcer items are available at lower prices when used? Are you playing philately as you would a ball game or are you using it for a diversion? If for a diversion, don't permit unreasonable demands to reduce your pleasure. Gear your quality requirements to your available funds. If later on you become richer, you can always upgrade your collection. In the meantime you have had the stamps that you enjoy. Isn't that better than only dreaming of the arrival of your shipment and having empty albums while you await its coming?

* * *

There is more beauty in most recent stamps of almost every country than in the older issues. Modern methods and machinery have made possible the production of multi-colored miniature art works at fantastically low cost and high speed. The slow, tedious labor of the nineteenth century engraver has been supplanted by photography. Paper, glue, ink and everything else has changed, from as recently as a generation ago.

All this catches the eye and emotion of millions of new collectors. It is good for the hobby, and yet from a personal viewpoint it leaves me cold. The lure of age, crudity, usage, historical association, social benefit and even economic struggle that faced our forefathers in their efforts to gather, study, classify and preserve the stamps of earlier days is to me the greatest attraction of philately. I would rather have a lot of nineteenth or early twentieth century to sort and study than any recently produced group of stamps. No matter what the country, I get a feeling of nostalgia for stamps that were rarely centered, often heavily cancelled and are frequently unavailable in very fine condition. These were the pioneers of our hobby. They carry the banner of the advance guard who as early as 1850 were scrounging their friends' wastebaskets for the bits of paper that brought messages from overseas. For me they will always be the lighthouses of philatelic lore.

* * *

This ad will apply to very few of my readers. Most stamp collectors are too wise to be of the few I am addressing. I am writing about those who through their enthusiasm, self-centeredness or just plain selfishness permit philatelic interests to ruin their marriage. I have always maintained that a man or woman is entitled to a good hobby and usually is a better person for having one, but as in all things, stamp collecting must be conducted in moderation. The family is deserving of its fair share of attention, time and company.

I have known collectors who almost every week in the year attend a stamp show. Sometimes this requires considerable travelling time.

When I see them always without their spouse I wonder about the consideration they give to their family life. Certainly the goal of those who put on the show is to get the greatest possible attendance but not at the cost of causing a family to go two different ways. I believe it is possible at the same time to enjoy stamp collecting and a happy married life. A person is twice as blessed if their mate is also a collector. However, if such is not the case, don't permit your hobby to blind you to the needs of companionship on the part of the other half. Don't think it right for you to go off alone a good part of your free time to stamp gatherings. Marriage is a partnership at which each member must work. Are you doing your share?

* * *

When an active, busy person is confined to bed by an illness, the passage of time becomes interminable. Long minutes stretch into even longer hours. Days seem to be a stretchout of weeks, and weeks resemble the month one spent in basic training some years ago.

It is at such a time that a good indoor hobby can be useful. One such as stamp collecting can be enjoyed by many people recovering from a wide variety of injuries. There are bed trays that provide a suitable album resting place, bed lights that provide good illumination and of course stock books of all sizes where you can tuck in stamps according to your classification scheme.

The time to acquire the stamps for such sick room use is now. We never know when we will need them. Therefore now, before an emergency, acquire and put away some good mixture or country collections or a batch of old covers. Hold it for the time when it can make the minutes, hours, days and weeks act normally in their passage through time.

* * *

In order to build a meaningful collection there should be a limit to what is collected. The time available and the funds that are likely will be first considerations in setting this limit. We all dream of a golden galleon sailing up to our house but few have ever had the experience of gazing upon such a wonder. If the job is a 50-, 60-, or 70- hour week routine, we must allow for sleep and other necessities so stamp collecting will be limited. When then to collect and how to establish the limits?

I believe that it is most important to have an emotional contact with your selected subject. If your ancestors were Swedish you could very well have feeling for that part of the world. If you earn your livelihood by baking French bread, that may direct you in another direction. It is good to have some connection with your choice of specialty. Before casting your lot with a subject look over the catalogs and literature that is devoted to it. Do they indicate a possibility of obtaining the material your collection will require? Can you afford the key items that will make yours stand above the run-of-the-mill efforts? Are you as yet sufficiently learned in the basics of stamp collecting to take the step of restricting your interest? The answers must be honestly considered before you cast yourself on the waters of advanced philately.

* * *

I recently wrote giving what I believe are some good reasons to collect postally used stamps. The week after I wrote those lines, a large accumulation of used U.S. gathered early in this century was brought to me from Europe. Needless to report, there was the usual percentage of off center and straight edges. Some were cancelled too heavily. The majority were nice collectable stamps and included all the Louisiana, Pan American, Jamestown and Panama-Pacific issues in quantity.

Just for the fun of it and proof of my "collect used theory," I sorted all the stamps, graded them for centering, discarded the damaged and arranged the lot by shade. It is really surprising how many shades exist of almost every stamp. To acquire them in unused condition is far beyond the means of most collectors but in selected used shape they fit into most budgets.

After a week or so of enjoying the task, I wound up with an attractive display of United States postage and commemorative issues with everything up to the one dollar value from 1890 to 1920. It was fun and I figure cost about 10% or 15% of what fine, unused with gum would cost. Shouldn't this be an inducement to many of you?

* * *

I just recently visited a highly successful stamp club where there were all kinds of activities except the one most needed. There were four dealers displaying their wares. The social hour table had coffee and cake. The officers and most members circulated, greeting old members and extending a welcome to the visitors. The speaker of the evening was up to his task, and entertained well. Everyone had a good time. What, then, was missing? The most required of all activities—a corner of the room devoted to solving problems and teaching procedures. You can call it a workshop where members and visitors could bring their problem stamps and covers to get ideas and help from fellow members. They could ask, "Can this perforation be right?," "Is this the doubleline water mark?," "Do you think this stamp is repaired?," "Where can I find this in the catalog?," "Should I break this block?," "Is this cover kosher?," "Is my hand lettering good enough to pass up using a lettering guide?" and any other of the questions that arise in stamp collecting.

We are apt to forget that it took us years to learn what we know and that every day there are new collectors without our long background of experience. To them, the most useful aspect of a stamp club is that it offers an opportunity to join with other collectors who can pass on words of guidance. This isn't to say that every stamp club has towers of philatelic learning among their members, but there is bound to be some wisdom that should be spread around.

If your club is not already providing a workshop, you should consider doing so. It is a service that will do much to increase the interest of new collectors in joining your organization.

* * *

There is no shortage of stamps. Dealers have enormous stocks of a wide variety. Even valuable items reside in the vaults of many dealers awaiting your order. What usually holds off your order is limited funds. I cannot help you to have more money, but I can advise you how to obtain the stamps you want with less delay. All I suggest is that you ignore the extreme fetish of condition that has received undue publicity lately. No one contends that a handsome, fat-margined stamp isn't going to sell for more than an average, run-of-the-mine example. The question is whether you can afford to join the club of collectors whose members regularly pay over catalog for everything they buy. How many of the stamps that you need for your collection can you buy at those rates?

Isn't it better to add to your collection and enjoy stamps daily than to await the exceptional and get something new once every six months? Philately is supposed to be a pleasant game. It is playable only if you have stamps to study and place in your collection. I'm heartily in favor of getting back to the standards of yesterday when it was expected that the stamp you bought today had been in someone else's collection before, and that the previous owner used hinges. I recommend nice looking, average stamps. They make your collection more handsome than do soiled ragged examples. You can have an attractive collection if you collect average material because it's available at fair prices. Those who seek the one in a million never will have a collection at all, because what they want isn't available often enough.

* * *

About half the world is in tropical or damp climate zones where stamps with gum readily become stained brown unless kept in an air-conditioned place. If collectors were realistic, they would expect items from humid areas to bear discoloration, but most collectors aren't realistic. As a result, they demand and get stamps of tropical origin that have never been to the country from which they are supposed to come. Stamp distributors or wholesalers get them directly from the printing works in Switzerland, England, France, Austria, etc. I may be considered strange, but I like my Sierra Leone or Brazilian stamps to have been on sale in the post offices of those places. What is Liberian about the product of an Austrian printer and a New York new issue merchant receiving his supplies directly from that printer? In the long distant past when postally cancelled stamps were the thing, most collectors would have rejected the majority of today's stamps as being labels only. Since the style now is for uncancelled we dealers cater to it, but shouldn't we demand that what we offer for sale comes from a legitimate post office in the country whose name is on the stamp?

* * *

To me, the Bicentennial of the United States seemed a far away thing on January 1, 1976. I was fortunately at Clearwater Beach, Florida, where the day was perfect. The temperature ranged between 60 and 70 degrees, the sky was cloudless and the breeze light enough to barely fill the sails of the numerous sailboats that passed back and forth on the bay. The day was so lovely that we who were here for a vacation could believe it was an omen of a wonderful year to come. There are few such days in a lifetime. Twenty-four hours with nothing to spend them on.

I think that stamp collectors get more than their share of the hours and days that are so perfect. They can on occasion draw a curtain around themselves and withdraw to whatever phase of history, geography, or topic that suits them at the time. They can enjoy being alone with their stamps even though there are others in the same room. Whatever the way they prefer to do their stamp collecting, it can be all absorbing. Enmeshed in its interests, the collector becomes oblivious to everything else. Thus philately can be the making of a perfect day as much as beautiful weather at Clearwater Beach. When blessings are counted, you can add many points for whatever it was that caused you to take up stamp collecting.

* * *

At the bottom of the Depression in 1934, our first auction catalog cost $57.50 to print. It wasn't much on appearance but it did the job of selling stamps and covers. Now, 49 years later, a recent catalog cost us more than $10,000 to print and to mail. That first sale grossed about $12,000—the recent one $595,000. That is quite a difference.

I was looking over the listings in that first catalog with the idea of guessing what they would bring today. Almost all the lots were United States covers. I suppose, on the average, they would sell for 20 times as much in today's market. Please remember that a dollar in 1934 was a fortune to many of the destitute people who were in the majority then. Today, a dollar is change when you break a twenty.

All philatelic material hasn't advanced in the same phenominal percentage as has desirable covers. The collector of today who soaks his stamps off the cover is a rare person. There is wide appreciation of the value of the stamp showing its usage, routes, time consumed, and all the other factors that might be found on a cover.

Recently, a man who lives in the Canary Islands sent to me his list of cover wants. He is striving to get a cover from every occupied part of the world. He still lacks such places as Somalia, Yemen and Confederate States of America. It will be a pleasure to help him complete his wants although a few will take time.

Another friend collects the same way but only one cover from a place and that the earliest item he can locate. As earlier dates show up, he sells off the later one thus keeping his cost down. There really is no limit to the things you can do in philately. Stamps can be collected in a system that you select and no matter how unusual it is, can provide you with joy for as long as you live. I remember with pleasure, my visits with the delightful elderly lady who collected only purple stamps. She referred to them as her bunch of violets. Think of how many other colors there are for those inclined that way.

* * *

Most people live uncertain lives, dependent on matters beyond their control. Under these circumstances, long-time planning is difficult. Even the most important activities—those dealing with health, shelter and sustenance—are frequently subject to the receipt of a regular paycheck. How then can we expect longrange planning of a hobby?

Most stamp collectors fabricate a dream of what they would like to accomplish with their collections. With some, it is to gain a certain size; with others, it is to earn prizes. Still others hope to make a profit from their collecting efforts. There must be hundreds of ambitions possible. Yet all of this can be dashed by a loss of a job, experiencing illness or any other of the chances imposed by life. You might then ask, why plan? Why dream?

Life is made up of plans and dreams. They are its sustenance as much as the food we eat. Without them, there comes an emptiness that is most apparent in some old people who have lost all hope. You may never come close to that dream of a gold medal in an international stamp show, or possession of blocks of Columbians, but as long as you have your collection you will have an incentive to keep plugging away on a course that adds great benefits to your life.

* * *

It is certainly pleasant to sit on the beach in a warm December sun and watch the boats go by. Those fortunate enough to be able to do this should be thankful. The people who live in the development where I spent last winter mostly are retired. They worked hard for many years and have well earned the sunset of life in pleasant surroundings and a comfortable climate. Many of them golf. There is tennis and shuffleboard available for those who like those sports. The community building houses playrooms for others who enjoy cards and crafts. Anyone who wants to can be kept busy from morning to night. All those who I have met continuously have things to keep themselves occupied. This constitutes a pleasant way of retirement.

As an added attraction to my "loafing," I have an interest in a grand hobby—stamp collecting. Not only has it been my life's work, it is my constant charmer. It chases away the darker clouds of living and admits to my ever increasing wonder a constant flow of color, ideas and learning. With it I have a gaiety far greater than that induced by the weather or good company. The collecting of stamps can continue even while sunning oneself on the beach because this is a place to contemplate the ideas gathered from the last look at one's albums.

The person who said, "Anyone with a good hobby lives in the best of two possible worlds," was certainly right.

* * *

How much should a stamp cost? With low-priced items, one must expect a minimum charge based on handling costs and the amount of time needed to furnish the item to the one ordering it. The minimum charge will vary from dealer to dealer but might justly amount to over catalog in many cases.

Then there are a vast group of stamps that are only slightly scarce but because of either face value or time required to locate them carry a basis cost. These are mostly in the range of 50¢ to $5 in catalog value. The quality factor enters into such stamps but to a lesser degree than in the case of rarer and less plentiful higher-priced items. Stamps in this middle ground—between plentiful and scarce—usually can be bought at a discount and it pays to shop for them.

Higher-priced and rare items almost always sell in accordance with their condition. Excepting the newer issues of the past twenty years, almost all have been in collections and can be expected to show hinge marks (not thins or damages). Since centering was more generally a problem of bygone times, it is more difficult to obtain in older stamps. Freshness, attractive cancellations, multiples, marginal imprints and richness of shade all count. An example is a stamp that is priced at $25; one place may have as a competitor for your money the item priced at $50 elsewhere. You must decide if the quality is worth the difference.

Care in buying pays off. And for goodness sake, never forget that after you buy you must use even greater care in seeing to it that your stamps are properly preserved.

* * *

Recently while at a friend's house, I looked over his fifty-volume collection of topicals. It included Kennedy, Space, Visitors, Maps and some other subjects that I had never even thought of. Most of the stamps were pretty and the mounting was attractive. From each collection I learned facts that had previously passed by me. No doubt the cost of the collection to my friend was considerable—the value of the albums alone ran into many dollars.

On the way home from my friend's house, I thought of the benefits and drawbacks of this type of collecting. They should be understood in advance by those who enter the field. Here are a few of my thoughts. Usually, topical collections are made up of odds and ends since complete sets are seldom applicable to a single topic. Those stamps that aren't applicable are ignored with a consequent loss of the learning that a broader form of collecting might yield. There is an almost complete lack of contact with early stamps, since in the main the early issues are not pictorials suited for division into topics. From a recovery viewpoint, topical collections usually realize a smaller percentage of catalog.

In favor of topicals are the points that usually perforations and watermarks can be ignored. Topicalists also point to the learning gained by the needed research into the subject. Some also claim that a good topical collection can be formed out of one's duplicates. After reading this you will decide for yourself. No matter how, be sure to have fun and enjoy learning.

* * *

From my observation, the most benefit from stamp collecting is gained by those who continue with the hobby for many years. It is a source of strength through all the stages of life and can always be relied on to bolster the spirits during dark days.

Those who continue collecting for a lifetime are usually further rewarded by the steady growth of value of their holdings. Even if profit was never the motive of a purchase, the years do raise the price of good stamps—sometimes phenomenally. I have seen many an old man who was amazed at the price offered for his collection. After all, the U.S. Columbian issue of 1893 was available in very fine condition in 1930 for about $100. The $1 Cattle in a Storm of 1898 sold for about $3.00

The better stamps of every country have shown stamp collecting to be a wise long term hobby. If only the fast buck boys who want to make a killing in a year would listen to old time dealers and make enjoyment their real goal. Then instead of the worry that they associate with stamps they would have contentment valued far beyond their cash outlay.

* * *

When I first heard of topical collecting sometime about 1932, I was quite surprised that anyone could enjoy other than conventional stamp collecting. For nearly a century the printed album arranged by country and date of issue had been king of our hobby. Now some upstarts were suggesting a radically different procedure—arranging by the subject matter of the stamp design.

Little did I know that this was but the beginning of a change that would eventually cause dealers to say, "No two collectors collect the same." Even if your specialty is plate number blocks, you probably have a quirk or two that makes your collection different. In any stamp club, the interests of members are so divergent that they often don't speak the same philatelic language.

This is all probably a good trend. The world of stamps is too huge for all of us to be likely to enjoy the same procedure. The man who collects all the shades of an issue so that he can break it down by printings is acquiring just as much benefit as the fellow who studies the engraving to detect constant varieties and flaws. Both are enjoying our hobby in the way that suits him. Since the purpose of a hobby is to add to the usefulness of leisure hours, this is good. None of us can foresee the trends of the future but for now, philately is healthy mainly because it is so variable.

* * *

There seems to be nothing else as inevitable as death. This isn't a topic that cheers but it is necessary to consider its implications. As I grow old and friends pass on, I am amazed that some of the most intelligent leave their affairs in the greatest mess. Unneeded taxes and legal fees deplete their assets until survivors sometimes receive only a fraction of what should have been their just inheritance.

If a stamp collection is part of your assets, have you provided good advice to your lawyer and executors about its disposal? Remember the dealers you patronize and the fellow collectors you know are probably strangers to them. Few lawyers are cognizant of the advantages of auction selling of stamp properties. Only a handful of trust officers have had experience in the philatelic world.

It is your obligation to be specific about what you want done with your stamps. If you want them to go to your grandson, say so in your will, but first consider his likelihood to become a collector. Also, wouldn't it be better for him to have to start a collection from scratch and enjoy all the new philatelists experiences. If you believe the collection to be a nest egg for your family's maintenance leave advice to have it converted to cash in the way you deem best. Finally, do not leave to chance that which you can assure. Your heirs deserve the best possible arrangement.

* * *

The chore of keeping philatelic cost records does not appeal to many collectors. Stamps are primarily for fun and certainly, bookkeeping is not fun. However, the Internal Revenue Service is a prying inquisitive branch of our government and it believes that profit on hobbies should be taxed.

To the best of my knowledge, few collectors keep an account of their expenditures for stamps. Most of the money goes for miscellaneous items and is unrecorded. Alas our government has no sympathy with such carelessness. When stamps are sold, records of cost and place of purchase are expected to be available so the suitable taxes if due can be levied.

I urge all collectors to set up a system that will make this information available whenever it is demanded by the U.S.I.R. It is the only fully convincing means of assuring that you won't be charged an unfair amount by an agent who makes an assessment on the seat-of-the-pants method.

The system does not have to be elaborate. You can devise one that suits your collecting habits. The point is to have it available if that fellow with the briefcase ever asks for it.

* * *

As collectables go—stamps are a comparative newcomer. After all, postage stamps invented in 1840 are only one hundred and thirty-eight years old. But let us pause a minute to consider what they have done for mankind and what collecting them can do for people. Through the almost universal use of postage stamps, a form of cheap and relatively assured communication has been set up all over the earth. After you have addressed and stamped your letter, no matter how remote the destination, the chances favor delivery within a reasonable time. The postage stamp has probably drawn the people of earth closer together than any other invention.

An added feature to the stamp is its use as a hobby that is both relaxing and educating. From it, we can acquire broader knowledge and improve mental health. Indeed during its brief existence many million collectors have obtained all the wondrous benefits to be found in "our bits of colored paper." There are many inventions that have made life more satisfactory on our planet. In my estimation, postage stamps must rank near the top of any list that attempts to grade inventions in proportion to their effect on and help to worldwide mankind.

* * *

If you are new at stamp collecting try this. Select a stamp—any stamp. Write down everything you can find out by examining it. Some of the things you will write are: the country of issue, the subject, the color, the size, the type and quality of paper, the inscription in the design, the denomination, the watermark if any, the size of the perforations and type of machine that made them, if unused the type and quality of the glue, the form of printing used—that is engraving, lithography or others.

You haven't as yet looked in a catalog, but already have a dozen or more facts about one little stamp. Can't you get the feel of the vast amount of knowledge to be gleaned from all the world's stamps. You will probably limit your collecting, but, in every section of philately there is much to learn. It's there asking you to absorb it.

From time to time I meet a collector who ignores all of this available knowledge, whose only joy in collecting is placing a stamp where it belongs and going on to the next item. It is against my principles to judge anyone's stamp collecting scheme, but sometimes I wonder if such collectors have ever had the great range of potential learning from philately called to their attention.

* * *

Economists are forever splashing their forecasts in newsprint and for the most part they are wrong. Seldom does the business world react as has been predicted. This is no reflection on individual economists. The fact is that the number of imponderables in our complex society make even the best forecasting a game of lucky guesses.

You might say that predicting anything is just as full of chance. No one can foretell with any certainty what the future holds. So why do so many stamp collectors delegate to investor advisory firms the selection of stamps to be acquired for future profit? I frequently wonder how the advisors can rest at night knowing that they have caused people to tie money up in stamps with no more likelihood of profit than that offered by the old time "blue sky" peddlers.

My advice to all collectors is—select a field of collecting. Try to acquire whatever items are useful in the enjoyment of that field. Buy them in the best condition you can afford. Preserve them from climate and other risks. Keep them a minimum of ten years. Then with luck and a good selection of the selling method, you should make out well, especially if you allow a percentage of your costs for enjoyment.

* * *

There is quite a resemblance between a close baseball game and the final judging at a stamp exhibition. The contestants in both cases have nervous tensions, apprehensions of possible bad luck, and when the final results are announced, either exhilaration or dejection. Of course in the ball game athletic skill can determine the result but more often it is luck. A batted ball can become either a hit or an out, depending on the position of the fielder. A display of stamps might be a silver or a gold, with the decision perhaps made by the judges' disposition on the day of judging.

Why then do some stamp exhibitors take such a serious attitude towards the result of the jury? It should be realized that there is no machine to make the decisions. The results are the record of the opinions of human beings at the particular time involved. The same jury might have an entirely different opinion a week later. The competitive exhibitions that get better or lesser awards than you do are not necessarily better or worse. It all depends on the objective of the collector plus the bias of the jury. The former is difficult to explain in an entry form and the latter totally unponderable. The luck of a baseball game is easier to understand.

* * *

I have just finished reading TIME, the weekly news magazine. It is quite a changed journal from the one I used to subscribe to. It has almost become a philosophical collection of essays. Gone is the straight reporting of news, events, sports, business, births, deaths and policies from all parts of the world. Yes, some of these things remain but far more space seems devoted to interpreting and applying historical relationships to events. The philosophizing about life is done in an interesting and generally easily understood style. I like the new TIME. I would like to see a monthly stamp magazine with a staff that could do a similar job of reporting and explaining things that go on in the philatelic world. Certainly, there must be meaning to the popularity of First Day Covers and the willingness of Americans to import tons of paper printed with the designs of various stamp issuing countries.

If we have thinkers who could interpret why some collectors are happiest when they are plating a stamp, let us enjoy reading about it. Perhaps the current rash of stamp investment firms could be explained and I for one would certainly like to know why anyone would buy several hundred new issues each year from each of the communist countries under the impression that they were needed postal issues.

The magazine I suggest wouldn't please everyone. Certainly not the speculator, the promoter of unnecessary issues, the fixer of fake coils or repairer of damages but we could gain by knowing more about them, their reasons for doing their thing and an understanding of the probable consequences.

* * *

The lad asked if we thought he should specialize. In reality he meant restrict his stamp collecting to a country or area of the whole. How could we give him good advice without knowing more about him. Some of the things that we should be familiar with are: how long he had been collecting, did he enjoy obtaining quantity more than completion of a limited part of his present album, and what was his potential for the future. We should know if he expected to go to college, what were his major interests, was he apt to put collecting completely aside during the boy-girl period of his life, could he afford to buy higher valued stamps that he would most certainly want in a restricted collection and most of all, had he learned from his general collecting the essential lessons of philatelic procedure. These are the care of stamps, an appreciation of the messages to be learned from them, the use of all the basic tools; perforation gauge, watermark detector, and various other helpful instruments. Was he able to tell the different types of paper used for printing stamps. Did he understand the several perforating methods, and quite importantly, had he reached the age where order and procedure were part of his life.

You cannot quiz a new acquaintance on all these matters. Neither can you offer good advice without having most of the answers. Therefore, in our wisdom, we asked the lad to visit us a few times and then we would offer him our guidance. Being a bright boy, he snapped at our offer. Today he is one of Philadelphia's outstanding young philatelists specializing in, of all things The Postal History of Great Britain.

* * *

The November A.S.D.A. show in New York was a great deal different from the early ones held at the old armory building. This year's show was elegant in its appearance. The aisles were spacious walkways where the crowds could amble at their own pace. The air was fresh and I venture to say fewer people had colds after visiting the show.

The A.S.D.A. has made great progress over a period of the last twenty years. From a small, weak organization centered around New York, it has become national. It trys to elevate the ethical standards of stamp dealing and promotes the hobby by conducting regional dealer shows. The membership has grown to include most of the active American dealers and they are from every state in the Union.

A strong professional organization is a boon to every trade. It helps set standards of behavior for its members and acquaints the public with the service available from the trade. Stamp collecting is no different. As long as its dealers are associated in an organization dedicated to the improvement of all philatelic activities our hobby will be in safe hands. Every active dealer should support the A.S.D.A. and every collector should be familiar with its standard of ethics.

* * *

During 1928-29, prices for stamps were high by the standards of that time. Of course those prices would be "give away" in today's market. Nevertheless, full and double catalog for very fine quality was the accepted rate then as it is now. New collectors flocked to the hobby and many dealers could only see glory in the future. Then in October 1929, the bottom fell out of the stock market. It was not long before people who were financially squeezed started to sell their collections to raise money. No dear friends, they did not sell at record breaking prices but compared to all other collectables, stamps had the best market. Rare book buyers and collectors of fine paintings completely left the market, but all through the depression there were buyers for stamps and it was not at give away prices for really fine material. Considering the increase in purchasing power of the dollar, the price of stamps really held up.

The reason for relating this is that we are today experiencing inflation that reminds me of 1928-29. I do not pretend to know if there is any similarity in the causes and effects, but, I can say with authority that there will always be a good market for stamps. Even the unemployed look for a good pastime and the shrewd capitalist recognizes the value that is always intrinsic in rare stamps.

* * *

Let us consider the stamps of a country that is neglected by many collectors. I refer to Colombia Republic. Since 1859, that nation has issued a large number of stamps. The national issues were supplemented by numerous stamps issued by the various departments of the republic. Until later times, Colombia was really a loose federation in which the states possessed great power including that of having their own postage stamps. In 1904, that was changed and the central government became supreme.

In so mountainous a land as Colombia, land communication is difficult and air mail was received as a blessing. The slow river boats of the Magdelena were replaced by man-flown Condors. The early mails of Colombia are a fascinating study. The regular issues of the nineteenth century vary from crude lithographs to include stamps that were colored by hand (some of cubiertas). Generally, early covers are scarce to rare. Postmarks, frequently manuscript, are quite interesting. The majority of items are in the middle price range. If fine condition is demanded, one must look long for even moderately priced stamps.

After the civil wars of the beginning of this century, Colombia settled down and issued some handsome sets. There are quite a few really rare items. Look through your catalog and you will agree that here is a great country for specialization.

* * *

Life has a way of disappointing. The good health that you have fades or the profit you expected does not reach the hoped for amount. The lady you love loves another more than you and the election that you thought was in the bag goes the other way. Parts of the Bible and much of philosophy accent the probability of these things and yet most of us enjoy life. We learn in our early days to accept the bitter with the sweet and smile through. Over the years, we construct a shelter to protect us from setbacks. With some it is religion, with others inner resourcefulness. Those who do not have a shelter are doomed to mental anguish.

Among the best shelters is an absorbing hobby and at the top of any list of hobbies is stamp collecting. Millions of people have learned that they can withdraw from their problems by opening an album or a box of unclassified stamps. In the more euridite levels of philately, the reading of a research article on one's favorite topic is sufficient to relax mind and body. It is no wonder that our hobby is so popular. No where else in life can the child for his twenty-five cents and the millionaire for his fortune, gain the same result—contentment.

* * *

During a recent visit to the Dominican Republic, I was informed that there were at most 100 collectors living there. Since there is a population of 5 million, that is a very small percentage. Why is this?

The low income of most of the people combined with poor educational levels makes the enjoyment of any diversion almost impossible. Many, many people are unemployed and underemployed. Cash is non-existant to many families. School facilities are limited, particularly in the rural areas. When crops are ready to be harvested, the kids must help the adults with the farm work.

Fortunately the present government is exerting considerable effort to help raise the standard of living. There is much construction under way, especially in respect to modern housing, and schools are opening everywhere. The future looks better.

I wonder what will happen to Dominican Republic stamps if the people there, aided by a raise in income and improved education, take a liking to stamp collecting. Suppose instead of 100 there were 10,000 Dominicans interested in collecting stamps of their native land. You can foresee the resultant sky-rocketing of prices.

This condition exists with many countries. Prices are low, not because the stamps are plentiful but due to the fact that the home market is weak. As income and educational levels become heightened in these countries, the stamps that are now slow-selling will be gobbled up in a booming home market. I almost cannot wait for those people to learn the great pleasures of philately.

* * *

It could be that you are at a crossroad in your collecting—that you would like to go ahead toward your goal of completing country X but everything missing from your albums costs a month's or more income. While you would gladly make the sacrifices needed to obtain those elusive stamps, you doubt if the wife and your mortgage holder would feel the same way. So what do you do? Let us look the situation over.

First—there is no rule of philately that states you must achieve completion. Second—somewhere in the collection that you have already amassed, there must be a section just dying to be further studied and specialized. Perhaps it can provide a long period of study and research for less cost than one of the stamps still missing from your albums.

Third—Philatelic knowledge isn't expanded by acquiring rarities. It grows from reading what others have learned and then using your own abilities to add to existent storehouses of learning.

Never consider a collection complete or beyond your ability to add to it. There is always one or more parts that can be as rewarding to additional study as was the original effort.

* * *

There are some really scarce stamps that list in the catalog for pennies. Sometimes it takes years to find one. To the casual collector this seems a strange condition. Scarce but cheap is contrary to the law of supply. Ah, but demand is also important and many stamps have little demand. There may be spaces for them in albums but general collectors don't especially seek them.

Sometimes the catalog makers know of a hidden supply of a stamp and hesitate to raise its price because that may cause the one holding the supply to flood the market. There are also known examples of government employees holding back certain denominations in the hope that later demand to complete sets will make for profitable deals. All together there are many ways in which relatively common stamps can be difficult to locate. These are not the object of this article. The stamps I refer to are in a separate class—scarce and low catalog price. Countries that are unpopular are most likely to be the place of origin of such items.

When a knowledgeable dealer asks you for a dollar for an item listing a dime, you better buy it. His experience could indicate that it might be a long time before he has another one for sale.

* * *

Almost all occupations are now specialized. The medical profession breaks down into hundreds of intensely detailed studies. The law is too complicated for general practice. Thus we have criminal, civil, admiralty, patent and other legal specialties each a nitch in which a lawyer can spend his entire life. Teachers, carpenters, plumbers and builders all tend to the branch of their work that suits their abilities.

Our readers are stamp collectors who just as any of the above craftsmen require a general familiarity with their subject as a foundation on which to build their selected section of philatelic life. Some never change from saving all stamps as they are available. A larger group restrict their collections to certain areas, periods or subjects. Then there are the few who become true specialists. They seek great learning and skill in a particular phase of our hoby and then apply themselves to forming a collection that demonstrates that knowledge. Philatelic specialization is just as intricate and demanding as specialization in any other human activity. It isn't for the casual collector or flitterbug who likes one topic now and another next month. It requires a tenacity and drive that most of us don't have.

I personally salute all who love stamps and research sufficiently to devote their minds towards adding to the enormous store of learning already existing about most branches of philately.

* * *

Every year disaster strikes many parts of the world. Floods, earthquakes, drought, epidemics and many other scourges affect millions of people.

The welfare of any and all of us can be the target of these calamities. There is no exemption. I think a tax to be levied throughout the world and used solely for disaster relief would be a good idea. It could be supervised by the United Nations and distributed by action of the World Court.

A way of collecting this tax could be a surcharge on postage rates for certain months in the year. All mail in every country during certain designated times would require an international tax relief stamp. Many millions could be raised by this method. It would be easy to control compliance and the funds being under the direction of the World Court would be equitably distributed. Almost everyone would be a contributor because there are few people who don't use mail service. A form of charity to which many contribute is good in that it spreads the blessings widely. It would enable people everywhere to say, "I do my share."

* * *

It may come as a surprise to many modern stamp collectors that at one time there were many times as many stamp stores as there are today. Cities of 100,000 population frequently supported a half a dozen stores earlier in this century. Now with emphasis on mail dealing and auctions plus the desire of many to purchase only the newest issues, so many stores would be beyond the economic market of successful operation. Collectors of the earlier period were accustomed to bringing their albums to the store and whenever they found a stamp they needed, filling the space. A visit to a dealer might take several hours. We still have a few such collectors, but by far the majority are busy men and women, in and out in five minutes. The dealer scarcely gets to know them, let alone give them the advice for which he was formerly sought out. Their sole object is to obtain a plate number block 39462 of the latest issue or a packet of mounts that will keep their stamps from contact with human hands. A few words about the elusive 3¢ Louisiana Purchase issue or the study of postmarks on 3¢ greens is not for them.

Certainly philately has room for all types, sizes and shapes of collectors. We welcome every one of them, but to all of them we say, "Open up your eyes and look around you." You will see a world you never saw when you had limited your vision to one small facet of stamp collecting.

* * *

Everyone has a different path through life. Some are smooth, others are rugged. However, there is never a completely rugged or completely easy path. Each of us has a share of easy living and difficult problems. How we handle the problems is the measure of the joy we can incorporate into our life.

It seems to me that those people who cultivate a variety of interests are in a better position to carry themselves through trying situations. They have something to fall back on when what they expect does not occur. If the trip to Europe proves impossible, they have another diversion that can fill in the time. Certainly, it may not be as exciting but it is there awaiting a call if the necessity arises. Such hobbies as stamp collecting, painting, creative writing, woodworking, etc. are worth cultivating if only to have a prop for a time when everything else seems to go to pieces. Then instead of self-sympathy, the hobbiest draws on his reservoir of other interests to fill in a gap or tonic his mind. It is then that a hobby is most appreciated and repays for all that has been put into it.

* * *

The winter of 1976–77 will go down in history as one of the coldest. The meteorological factors that caused this are not completely understood but the effect on people is severe. There was widespread cancellation of meetings, travel and even factory closings due mostly to fuel shortage.

A couple of stamp collectors I know thought all of this was great. It gave them more time to devote to their albums. They said, "If you cannot go out, the television programs are boring and the family conversation runs out, what is better than to be a stamp collector with stamps to study and place in the albums." I agree. The only catch in the statement is the part about having stamps to study and place where they belong. Too many collectors neglect to keep such a backlog. They do not realize the value of an unsorted box of loose material or a batch of miscellaneous covers—the kind that can be bought in almost any auction. Certainly, the chances are that there will be nothing in the lot to add to your collection but you have really purchased diversion time activity. You might have even learned a thing or two from items that do not fit into your collecting scheme. The next time you see such a lot offered, try to buy it, you never can tell when it will make the sun shine on a dreary afternoon.

* * *

Everyone has received a cheery "Have a nice day," upon parting from even the most casual acquaintances. It's part of the present American scene and indeed a nice one—quite an improvement on the ordinary "Goodbye." Few of those who use this saying have any idea how everyone should go about having a nice day. Should we devote some time to reflection or prayer? How about the swindlers among us? Should they put forth additional effort to acquire the possessions of others unlawfully. Yes, "Have a nice day," has many interpretations. For me, at present, it means have several hours of free time to delve in the boxes and files of unsorted stamps that I own. For me it means to continue the hope that somewhere in each box I will find some long hidden gems. What a nice day I will have if my hopes come true.

Stamp collectors and all others are urged to always have nice days. It might be suggested that good planning will make them more likely. Plan for the days that are coming so that you will always have some really pleasant activity to mix in with the seemingly unpleasant or repetitious jobs we all must do.

* * *

I have a couple of close friends who go fishing every day for the sport of the thing, usually without catching a single fish. They sit in their boat and dangle lines that they hope will attract the species of fish they enjoy eating. I estimate that they spend about fifty hours a week this way. Since they enjoy the pastime and it is apparently harmless, except to the fish, I am all for it.

However, I would like to compare this fishing with stamp collecting, an equally absorbing and relaxing hobby. There are few collectors who devote fifty hours a week to the hobby, but no matter how short or long the time everyone of them closes his albums with a measure of additional learning, something that I doubt most fishermen gain. And for excitement, how can one compare the landing of a fish with the discovery of a new variety or the completion of a stubborn set of stamps. Sure I am biased. Who wouldn't be after 64 years of collecting?

* * *

Somewhere today there are men and women starting a stamp collection. If I could give them a few words of advice, I would concentrate on the need to become familiar with the basics of our hobby. There is no substitute for understanding how to carefully handle stamps, the various terms used to describe them and how to recognize all accepted differences.

To my mind the best way to learn these basics is to form a worldwide collection of relatively common stamps. Each stamp placed in your album will be a reinforcement of your understanding of the "how and why" of stamp collecting. Of course, the collection will have little or no value, but after placing several thousand stamps in their proper place, you will have acquired the know-how to proceed with any philatelic subject you choose.

* * *

Do you remember your first stamp album? I remember mine. It cost $1.20, an amount that I accumulated by almost two months of economy such as walking to school and then saving the nickel that the trolley would have cost me. The album was in the window of a small stamp store and I passed it longingly for many a day ever hoping that it wouldn't be sold before I could afford it. When the magic day came, I floated home on a great white cloud.

The inducement or premium that went with the album was a stamp that catalogued all of a dollar. For some time, it was my great pride to point such a rarity out to my friends. When I later learned that in reality it was a worthless Nicaragua reprint, I realized what fun being ignorant can sometimes create.

No doubt most of my readers have equally pleasing memories of starting their first stamp collection. Along with sports, stamp collecting is a hobby of statistics and reminiscences. May it ever be thus, because while its ramifications can embrace every known branch of learning it is the personal experiences that endears philately to all of us.

Conducting a large stamp business can at times be trying. Some of the little thrills of the early days can be lost—but I hope there never comes a time when such things as a first look at a fine collection or finding a scarce variety in a mixed lot fails to excite all of us at Apfelbaum's.

* * *

The nation is turned into a center of philatelic shows—dozens of them every weekend in all corners of the country. Attendance is excellent and there is no doubt that millions are now exposed to our hobby where only a few years ago, outside of the big cities, there was an occasional stamp event to captivate them. This then is our great opportunity to tell our story.

We have brought philately out of the back rooms into shopping centers, convention halls and the leading hotels. Now we must add glamour to those shows that consist only of rows of frames and dealers bourse tables. How about signs that sell the idea of attending the symposiums and lectures that are now part of every show. The new collector and novice would seldom realize that these are for him as well as the more established philatelists. How about some effort to compose a catchy stamp collectors' march or song to be played at the opening of the show—and what would be the result of a corps of trained guides to give individual tours of the frames to all new or non-collectors who attended.

There are dozens of ways in which we can add recruits to our ranks that can be used at little cost to the organizations that put on our shows. Now is the time to use them—while the public is curious about one hobby.

* * *

My father had a stamp collecting friend Phil, whose entire philatelic activity was wrapped around his stamp tongs. The tongs had come from Europe years before as one of his prize possessions. He would speak long and loud about their perfect balance and he seemed to give mystical power to what he called "their care of my stamps."

Well, as will happen with all our possessions, there came a day when the tongs were missing. Phil searched his house from top to bottom to no avail. The result of the loss was extraordinary. Dad's stamp collecting pal ceased being a collector. He decided that he could never safely handle stamps with any other tongs so he put his albums up on the shelf and discontinued paying his stamp club dues.

Several months later he stopped to see my father about some business other than stamps. Dad was sorting out a pile of 3-cent 1851's and Phil his friend watched for awhile. All of a sudden he jumped up, let out a yell and grabbed Dad's tongs from his hand. "Where did you get these?" he asked. "They are my lost pair." Of course Dad had no idea where they came from. He had 100 pairs around the office. Probably Phil had left them there on a long forgotten visit. The sequel is that Phil returned to his collecting and even won the grand award in the next Philadelphia stamp exhibition.

* * *

The worries of evening are usually unimportant the next morning. Somehow laying awake long after sleep was due becomes a waste in the light of sunrise. Our country seems to bounce from crisis to crisis—largely promoted by ardent news media seeking a market for their wares. Think back over the past few years. You will agree that our time of instant news via radio and television has prompted many of our society's more extreme reactions. Perhaps slower dissemination of accounts of happenings would have given us more time to consider and to act wiser.

The stamp collecting world is not unlike the whole world. We hear of many things that are disturbing. The weekly stamp newspapers are constantly seeking items to fill their headlines. When these recount practices that most of us deplore, we are apt to become excited and demand remedial action from our societies. We demand less souvenir sheets or better first day cover service. We call for a boycott of certain issues or jail for an unidentified group of stamp fixers.

Time always remedies these problems. Few of us can recall what aroused us five or ten years ago. Life in its grand procession leads us away from last night's bad dream and into the one that we will have tomorrow night.

* * *

Stamp collecting is primarily for fun and learning. Without these two factors, it would soon die out. The pleasure of inspecting new acquisitions, placing them in the albums and studying their designs has for almost 150 years kept our hobby at the top of all diversions.

Some collectors worry because they don't see many children at stamp gatherings. They ask, "Where are the collectors of tomorrow to come from if we don't interest today's kids?" The truth is that this question was asked 25 and 50 and 75 years ago. Somehow the new collectors materialize. Philately is stronger today than ever, and its future was never brighter. It now attracts a broader spectrum of society; it offers its followers a greater range of material, and its dealers have stronger capitalization than ever before.

If you have doubts about who will be collecting fifty years from now, I assure you that those of us who were active in 1928 had the same concern. In those days, a nice U.S. #1 cost all of $5. Look at what it regularly sells for now and forget your worries.

* * *

I have just returned from a short trip abroad. I traveled with a group of about sixty people, only two of whom were admitted stamp collectors. However, everywhere we went all the people sought out the post office to buy stamps for friends and relations back home.

Stamps make a fine souvenir and interesting gift to bring back, but there should be some knowledge of collector's desires used in purchasing them. Almost everyone bought only the low values. One man bought only blocks but balked at the cost of the top values. For his expenditure, he could have obtained a complete set of singles, certainly a more desirable item than the blocks he bought. A lady had each stamp cancelled on the theory that it would prove she had been in the country of origin.

The collectors who asked these nice people to get them some stamps in the countries visited should investigate the availability and cost of current stamps from new issue dealers. They frequently could save money and certainly would be more likely to get exactly what they want from such a source than from unlearned shoppers at foreign post office windows.

* * *

One of my sharpest memories is of buying from the great dealer, Eugene Klein, about 1938, a two-volume specialized collection of Hejaz & Nedj. It included numerous errors and rare items. I paid him $200 for the collection. I never did find a buyer for it and sometime in the 1950's I gave it to the National Philatelic Museum, receiving a good tax deduction credit for it.

This was truly a good lot of stamps that are quite different from those of Western nations. The lack of a market was to me regrettable because there was much to be gained from collecting stamps of Arabia.

Everyone knows what has happened to this part of the world, how it has become important in many ways. The stamps that I then couldn't sell would today bring me a few thousand dollars. I didn't hold them long enough. But this is the history of all stamps—be patient and Mother Popularity will come around to everything sooner or later.

* * *

There are few, fortunately a very few, collectors who believe they can outfox dealers when they offer their stamps for sale. Perhaps once in a while one of them succeeds but generally any professional with even modest experience quickly sees through the false front of such tricksters.

A favorite of these fellows is to state a catalog value for their holdings far in excess of reality. Another gambit is to declare with a straight face that all their stamps are Very Fine when even a glance indicates scrubby items, repairs and tampered with material.

These tricksters generally do no harm. The world they live in is glamorized for them by their exaggerations. Only when, by misrepresentation, they cause a prospective buyer to travel out of his way on what turns out to be a waste of time, have they done actual harm. Then, in all honesty, they should pay for the travel and time of the dealer they have misled, but if they had that kind of ethics, they would not have misled him in the first place.

* * *

There are people who expect a financial return commensurate with their contribution from every activity in which they participate. They cannot understand recompense in the form of accomplishment for accomplishments sake. The doing of something in order to experience what it will teach or the well being it can engender is beyond their understanding.

Stamp collecting is an example of an activity that pays off far more in useful benefits than in dollar profit. Certainly there are many collectors who make a financial gain from our hobby but quite often they are the collectors who had no such motive. Purchase the stamps that will enhance your collecting pleasure. Study and enjoy them. Take good care of them and time will take care of your financial return. When years from now your material comes on the market it will realize its value as of that future date. Hopefully, this will be more than it cost you but if you allow for the fun you had the result is a certain profit.

* * *

The current never hinged craze brings to mind a Mr. P.D. who was for many years the outstanding collector in Philadelphia stamp circles. He was a real philatelist with great knowledge of all classic issues. His condition standards drove local dealers mad. Nothing but perfection interested him. "Price is no object—just get me the best," was what he impressed on each of the many stamp store owners that then graced our city. He exhibited regularly always to win a top prize and his talks to stamp clubs were gems.

About 1940 I noticed that he was selecting from my stock stamps with hidden faults; small thins, no gum, or other flaws but always something that couldn't be seen when the stamp was mounted. I questioned him about the change in his standards. He explained that he didn't care what his stamps would realize after his death. He never saw a judge in a show demand to inspect the backs of his stamps and he had concluded that he was a chump to pay several times as much as he needed to for a quality that went unobserved by anyone that looked at his collection.

* * *

I believe that some time ago, I wrote about the idea of a resort where stamp collectors could spend their vacation together with many other philatelists. These could be regional and if well run could result in fine business for their owners.

If a hotel or motel complex let it be known that stamp collectors constituted a good portion of its guests and that a room was provided for meetings, a fair philatelic library was on the premises and such items as slide projectors and black lights were available, I think that it would be a landmark to which philatelists would gravitate.

The summer vacation is a fixture in American life. What would be better than spending it at a place where you would know in advance that there would be others with similar interests and that the non-collecting members of your family would not be at loose ends for entertainment.

Some resort hotel or motel owner who is seeking to build his business on a firm foundation could start a very interesting trend by developing this idea.

* * *

We all know many collectors who have turned from general worldwide philately to restricted or specialized collecting. In fact, that is the accepted path of progress through our hobby. At least I thought so but now I am learning otherwise.

Several stamp collectors who have been at our hobby for many years have revised the program and after being specialists who formed fine and often prize winning collections have returned to gathering the world in their albums. They contend that memory of the great fun of their beginning days has urged them in that direction.

None of these people expect to come anywhere near the worldwide completion. In fact there are many stamps that they purposely omit from their albums. A few of them have eliminated watermark varieties because they are generally not visible except in fluid. Others have given up on perforations and stick to face different. The most sophisticated only take stamps that they like and here is a rule that certainly is elastic enough for anyone.

One of the greatest of the worlds philatelists once told me that if he wasn't worried about his reputation, he would resume general worldwide collecting because that was to him most pleasurable. Now some brave souls are disregarding opinions and doing what they enjoy most. After all, isn't that the first purpose of a hobby?

* * *

One interesting collection that I have seen is a study of ordinary first class mail postage rates. The one who formed the collection traced from the beginning of stamps the rates that would carry a letter internally to various parts of each country. He illustrated this with the stamps issued for the purpose and with covers when they were available to him. Issues of stamps that paid for extra weight letters, registry, special delivery and all the other special categories listed by Scott, Minkus, etc. were eliminated.

Surprisingly, he had a great story told graphically for each country. In the beginning there was a gradual reduction in the cost of sending a letter. It reached the level of two cents in the United States for several decades. Then in 1932, it started climbing until it is now higher than at any time since 1847 when our government started selling stamps to prepay postage.

This is just one of the interesting ways to form an unusual collection. I'll bet there are easily over 1,000 others.

* * *

I know it is unnecessary to call your attention to the complicated, exasperating, condition of present day life. You all know and experience it every day. What I want to remind you of is the quiet, uncomplicated, soothing time you experience when you are with your stamp collection.

You must have long ago realized the difference between the clang and the clamor of news reports of what is going on in the world and the pace that comes to you from your hobby. That is why you are a devoted philatelist. There are only a few avocations that are so completely absorbing that while one pursues them the care and problems of life fall away.

We in stamp collecting have one of the greatest of avocations. It educates while it entertains, it justifies its cost by great returns to those of its followers who are judicious. To those who have discovered it in its grandest form, that is the collecting method that best suits them, stamp collecting is one of the finer things in their life.

* * *

Do not be concerned if your collection is not the best in your stamp club. The first purpose of collecting stamps is to gain relaxation and learning, not to win exhibition prizes. Measure your philatelic activity by the things it does for you. Then there will be so much in its favor that you will appreciate the great asset that being a stamp collector can be.

A friend who really enjoys the contacts that collecting brings with other collectors has told me that even if he did not possess a single stamp, he would regularly go to philatelic activities. He claims that the excitement and the friendliness of people with kindred interests would never be equaled in other social contacts.

Those of you who are solitary collectors, who never visit a show or the local club are missing much that our hobby has to offer. Aside from the learning to be gained, you are almost certain to find people who will develop into long-time warm friends based on your liking similar things. Your horizons of other activities that you do will expand while you make stamp friends. The collector who strikes up a conversation while you both inspect a frame at the club exhibition can turn out to be an important local personality or better yet, someone who has much to offer you in the way of stamp guidance.

Enjoy as fully as possible all aspects of our fine hobby. You might not become a great philatelist but you will most certainly broaden yourself in many respects as you travel the stamp collecting path.

* * *

I cannot put too much emphasis on consideration of the problems in philately caused by excessive speculation. During my more than fifty years of stamp dealing there have been about seven times when people really not interested in collecting have caused price runups not warranted by supply or scarcity. Such increase in selling price is always rapid. It is accompanied by many names never before heard of suddenly becoming professional advisers, portfolio managers and touts of their personal records in making huge profits for the unwary. After a year or two you will never hear of these people again because their forecasts on which they alone profited have followed the proverbial bubble and burst.

A slow gradual increase in the worth of all good stamps may legitimately be expected by stamp collectors. Perhaps a dozen times a year a sleeper may be exposed as being underpriced and due for a phenomenal raise in selling price. Never, never does the entire market suddenly surge upwards except when the touts gang up and using "blue sky" methods cause large numbers of non-collectors to buy at continually increasing prices. At the proper time the touts withdraw and the investor/speculators have a file of stamps that within weeks have receded to their normal selling price.

Why do I worry about the speculators? Because when they try to unload their holdings to established and honest dealers they will claim all stamp collecting is a fraud based on what they are offered for goods that were never worth what it cost them.

* * *

Few of us realize how young our country is. In number of years, it now is 207 since the signing of the Declaration of Independence. This translates into the fact that my great-grandfather could have taken part in the signing celebration. Coming to an event that is closer, I had a grandfather who was alive at the time postage stamps were introduced—1840. Compare these facts to the history of most European countries and you will realize how young we are. Just think, if our grandparents had been stirred by the new invention of prepaying postage by stamps and had become collectors, we would have been in line for possible great wealth and surely for some interesting additions to our present holdings. I knew both my grandfathers and can testify that their lack of foresight in not being stamp collectors was in line with their not buying the right real estate or saving uncirculated four-dollar gold pieces for present day members of the family.

* * *

There have been quite a few excellent women philatelists but they are outnumbered many times by men. Since stamp collecting is a diversion that in no way can be unladylike, it is surprising that more of the fairer sex haven't taken it up and excelled in it. Let us go back a couple of generations and try to understand the reasons behind this. When I was a boy collector almost all the stamp clubs I knew were for males only. Women didn't apply and if they had they would have been rejected. There were several reputed, advanced, lady collectors in Philadelphia but they were outside the social contacts of the hobby. I recall only one lady who was accepted into a local club at that time, a Mrs. Mary Garretson Cook who specialized in Egypt.

Naturally, club exclusion meant exhibition exclusion and thus there was a body of male collectors who convinced themselves that philately was for men only. They almost forced the ladies to collect in the closet of secrecy.

All that is changed now. One wonders how the exclusion lasted as long as it did, but at the same time, we are very glad that in philately today sex doesn't count.

* * *

This will be a plea on behalf of the collection of postally cancelled stamps. Most of you have noted the steep climb of prices for unused stamps, particularly if they are in prime condition. Items that you would like to add to your albums have passed beyond your maximum for the purchase of individual philatelic pieces. The space that remains empty because you cannot afford to fill it can become a heartache. I for one would rather see a handsome used stamp in that spot than a black square that signifies "I cannot swing for this one."

To go further in my argument, I know that there is much more elasticity in price possible for used items and here again is the oldest cliche of all, when they bear postal cancellations, they have done the service for which they were created.

* * *

I know that many small and poor countries latch onto the issuance of stamps as a means of gaining income for their governments. It is probable that some could not exist otherwise. The generosity of stamp collectors provides almost the entire income of these places. It might be called a form of international charity for stamp collectors to support these places.

I would urge such "countries" to issue stamps that publicize their own history and economic resources. It is unbecoming for a West Indies island to commemorate world wide events that have no possible connection with the island. Collectors can be persuaded to collect stamps that inform them of events and things past and present that happened to the people of a place. It isn't necessary for a South seas country to issue a long set because a European sports team won a match of which the south seas place had neither representation or a local news report.

* * *

They called him "Frenchy" at the club. That wasn't his name, but he was such a storehouse of knowledge about anything from France, that his name was most appropriate. No one ever saw his stamps, in fact it couldn't be remembered when he last bought any at the club sales or local dealers. He was to some extent an eccentric who lived alone in a rented room, grafted meals from his friends, and used the Free Library for passing most of his leisure time. At last, as it happens to all of us, he passed away. A few of the collectors from the club went to the funeral. There they met his sister, and asked about his collection. They were surprised by her answer, "My brother never collected stamps," she said. "He enjoyed your company and meetings all those years more than anything else he ever did, and French, no he was born in Rome, Italy; I didn't know he was interested in France." With some inquiry at the library, it was revealed that he had read everything about his adopted interest in France.

This proves that you cannot tell a collector by his attendance at stamp club meetings.

* * *

The Philadelphia area recently suffered a great loss when Bertram Korn, a leading reformed rabbi, a great historian and an admiral in the United States Navy, passed away. His interests were as varied as the weather of our fair city. He warmly entered the hearts of those who knew him. Through his research and writings, I have learned much about the early history of our country, particularly the part played by the Jews.

This man was engaged 100% of his waking hours by the tasks he undertook. Leading a large synagogue is in itself a full-time job. In addition, he found time for his research and writing, for lecturing in many places, for his naval service and, I am proud to say, his stamp collecting. He was interested in and collected Arctic philately long in advance of the current popularity of that branch of our hobby.

What this all proves is that a busy man can always find time for more activity; it is only the person who is in a rut that never has time.

* * *

If the price of a stamp you want to purchase doubles during the time your income also doubles you are doing what is called keeping pace with inflation. It is when one part of this duet either remains stagnant or changes differently than the other part that things get out of balance.

During a time of the fluctuation of the purchasing power of money there are those who gain by being ahead of the change and those who lose by tardiness. Few of us stay in perfect balance.

We, philatelists, would be in a sad way if all stamps were still selling at the prices and discounts of 1970. Some few varieties that were overpriced then are still available for the old prices but any sound and semi-scarce or scarce stamp today commands at least double what was asked for it ten years ago. Some items, mostly rarer material, have increased much more than 100%. For this I am glad, but I ask those who get excited about it to also consider the current price of shoes, ships, and sodas. They should also take a long look at their income, their tax and the cost of a new family car.

* * *

What makes a good Apfelbaum's Corner? In my estimation, it is a piece that excites some collectors enough for them to turn to their albums and put some time in arranging or studying their material. My firm, the business that pays for these brief columns, is content with the results, no matter what stamp dealer may gain from what I write. It all balances out over the years and along with XYZ Stamp Company, we will gain more business if stamp collectors are prompted to spend more time with their albums.

I believe that the only way you can successfully take anything out of an activity is if you put as much or more back into it. This is my way of putting back into philately. It does not include intensive, detailed studies of a particular subject—or claims that only Apfelbaum's pays the highest prices. It neglects the hundreds, maybe thousands, of facts I have learned of particular philatelic subjects. All it does is try every week of the year to pep up your interest in stamp collecting. Apfelbaum's will take their chances on who will get your business. I've tried not to be self-serving, but to only serve our hobby.

* * *